CRIMSON

HARVARD ALUMNI
and
The Medal of Honor

by

Philip A. Keith

Harvard College, Class of 1968

Table of Contents:

(* New chapters in this Second Edition)

Author's Introduction (2nd Edition):

In 2010, a classmate sent me an intriguing article from the *Harvard Gazette* about a plaque, newly installed at Harvard's Memorial Church, honoring the Harvard Alumni who have been awarded the nation's highest award for military valor, the Medal of Honor. My friend guessed that as a fellow Harvard graduate, veteran, and writer of military books, I might be interested in the subject matter of the piece. He was right.

As I researched the stories of the men whose names are etched on that plaque, I uncovered fascinating tales about a group of truly remarkable individuals. The list of honorees had started with ten fairly well known citations, then quickly jumped to seventeen as publicity about the dedication of the new tablet was disseminated. An eighteenth citation was unearthed before the stone carver's tools had finished their work. Are there more stories that have yet to be uncovered? Possibly; but, a complete review of the records of the Medal of Honor Society, the best data resource on MOH awardees, cross referenced to the database of Harvard Alumni indicates we have the complete and current list (but not all war records are totally comprehensive, especially the older ones). New names could be added in the future since—as they always have—Harvard alumni continue serve our nation in all branches of the military. There is extra space on the beautiful Vermont, green marble stone for this possibility.

The eighteen Harvard recipients we know about served in almost every conflict since the Medal was authorized (1861). The MOH has been awarded 3,506 times as of the revising of this edition of "Crimson Valor." Almost half of the recipients (1,522) were from the Civil War; nineteen men were honored twice; there is one woman among the honorees; and seventy recipients, or thereabouts, are alive as this book goes to press.[1]

The record of incredible bravery and personal sacrifice of those who have earned the Medal is a glowing testament to the patriotism that characterizes the American spirit. Recipients have come from every corner of America, all walks of life and every uniformed service (Army, Navy, Marine Corps, Air Force, and Coast Guard).

As might be expected, many Medal of Honor recipients have had professional military training. Eighty-three West Pointers have been awarded the Medal of Honor; seventy-three have come from Annapolis; one from the Air Force Academy (The Air Force did not have a separate service academy until 1959). Other colleges and universities, public and private, have alumni who have received the Medal; but, it turns out that Harvard's total of eighteen is the longest list except for the USMA and the USNA. This remarkable record of *"Crimson Valor"* is the subject of this book.

Phil Keith
Southampton, NY
2011 (revised 2019)

---

[1] All statistics relative to the Medal of Honor are as of the date of publication of this book and courtesy of the Congressional Medal of Honor Society, http://www.cmohs.org

Chapter 1: A Brief History of the Medal of Honor

Military pomp and pageantry, gaudy uniforms, and all manner of gold braid, decorations, and medals were anathema to the nascent American military. Just as the Founding Fathers did not want any American kings, neither did they favor a standing army (or navy). They knew, of course, that in times of crisis martial methods would be required, but they vested most of their early military efforts in the care of the various state militias.

Federal forces were kept miniscule on purpose. Plain, mostly dark blue uniforms, characterized the Army and Navy in the early years of the nation and were worn with modest gold buttons and badges of rank. There were none of the pretentious baubles resplendent on so many European tunics. Medals smacked of pomp and privilege and were entirely contrary to the egalitarian image that the fledgling United States wanted to project.

There was one small exception. General George Washington wished to recognize exceptional gallantry or meritorious service within the ranks of his Continental Army: He tried to advance an officer or common soldier at least one rank whenever a noble or extraordinary deed was performed by that individual. The Army was so poor, however, and funds so tight, that the Continental Congress in 1782 forbade Washington from continuing meritorious promotions on the grounds that it would increase the payroll. The Commander in Chief felt that valor still needed to be rewarded; so, he struck upon an alternate plan. He devised a simple purple cloth badge, in the shape of a heart, with the word "Merit" stitched upon it.   Men who earned the badge, the predecessor to today's Purple Heart medal, would be allowed to sew it over the left breast of their uniforms. There are only three instances of these first Purple Heart awards on record, but it was the beginning of a new tradition and a tiny crack in the stone wall against the implied ban on medals and decorations for members of the American military.

By 1861, the United States was engaged in a vast conflict, an enormous enterprise that would require the recruiting and enlisting of millions of officers and private soldiers. At the beginning of the Civil War, the Regular Army had less than 16,000 men. Soon there would be gigantic corps structures and even separate armies within the army, formations the size of which the United States military had no practical experience managing.

As the conflict wore on, the men in each regiment, brigade, corps, and army began to take great pride in their outfits, many of which were regionally based. A popular groundswell arose favoring the adoption of a number of distinctive items of recognition among the differing units. At the brigade and regimental levels, uniforms started to sprout accoutrements such as deer tails (the 143rd Pennsylvania Bucktails Regiment), unit numerals, and special hats. At the larger corps levels, distinctive badges were designed. There were multi-colored shoulder straps for officers of the various branches within the Army: The artillery straps were red, the infantry blue and the medical corps green. Who could forget the famous Zouave Regiments with their bright-red, baggy pants and fez-style hats? Medals could not be far behind and, indeed, they were not.

"On December 9, 1861 Iowa Senator James W. Grimes introduced S. J. R. No. 82 in the United States Senate, a bill designed to 'promote the efficiency of the Navy' by authorizing the production and distribution of 'medals of honor'. On December 21st the bill was passed, authorizing 200 such medals be produced 'which shall be bestowed upon such petty officers, seamen, landsmen, and Marines as shall distinguish themselves by their gallantry in action and other seamanlike qualities during the present war' (Civil War). President Lincoln signed the bill and the (Navy) Medal of Honor was born. Two months later on February 17, 1862 Massachusetts Senator Henry Wilson introduced a similar bill, this one to authorize the President to distribute medals to privates in the Army of the United States who shall distinguish themselves in battle. Over the following months (the) wording changed slightly as the bill made its way through Congress. When President Abraham Lincoln signed S.J.R. No. 82 on July 12, 1862, the Army Medal of Honor was born."[2]

The Medal of Honor was initiated by Members of Congress and is generally awarded by the President "in the name of Congress;" therefore, it has sometimes been referred to as the Congressional Medal of Honor. This nomenclature is, in fact, incorrect. The official name of the award is simply the Medal of Honor.

The Medal of Honor was, at first, a "soldier's medal." It was intended to be awarded solely to navy enlisted men and petty officers or army private soldiers and non-commissioned officers (corporals and sergeants). By 1863, however, award of the Medal was extended to commissioned officers. The Medal of Honor was the only officially recognized Federal decoration on the books during the Civil War and it became greatly prized.

---

[2] Ibid

Post war, and to protect its integrity, a Medal of Honor Legion was established (1890) and this was followed by a Presidential order, from President William McKinley (a Civil War veteran himself) directing the Army to establish new regulations in regard to awarding the Medal. From 1897 forward, awards were made under the following guidelines:

"...Gallantry and intrepidity above and beyond that of one's fellow soldiers...

...Required that a submission for the Medal of Honor be made by a person other than the veteran who had performed the heroic deed...

...Required the testimony, under oath, of one or more eyewitnesses to the heroic deed...

...Set a time limit of one year for any person to be submitted for the Medal of Honor for an act occurring after 26 June 1897." [3]

Still, the Civil War legacy lingered, and some of the most belated Medals of Honor for living honorees were not bestowed until 1917, fifty-two years after the conclusion of the war. Indeed, three of Harvard's Civil War medalists (Blackmar, Porter, and Huidekoper) were not presented with their Medals of Honor until 1897, 1902 and 1905, respectively.

Remarkably, Civil War MOH awards are still being authorized. The latest were approved in 2001 and 2014. President Clinton conferred a posthumous MOH on Color Sergeant Andrew Jackson Smith for his bravery at the Battle of Honey Hill, South Carolina, on November 30, 1864. Smith, of the 55th Massachusetts Colored Regiment, was cited for

---

[3] Ibid.

carrying the flag throughout the battle after the original color bearer was shot down.[4]

On November 6, 2014, President Obama bestowed a posthumous MOH on First Lieutenant Alonzo Cushing, 4th US Light Artillery, Battery A, for his fearless and ultimately fatal defense of his guns in the face of Pickett's Charge, Gettysburg, July 3, 1863. Will Cushing's MOH be the last for the Civil War?

The Civil War MOH total could have been much higher had not a sloppy clerical error of 1863 been corrected (years after it occurred, in 1917): Another 864 Civil War MOH awards were made to the men of the 27th Maine. Three hundred of the regiment's members volunteered to extend their enlistments in June 1863, at a time when manpower was crucial and recruitment goals were falling short. Secretary of War Edwin Stanton had enticed these men to extend their enlistments by promising them the Medal of Honor. Somehow, a War Department clerk mis-read the order and gave the award to every member of the regiment—864 men in all.

Criteria for the award and standards for honorees continued to evolve, even after the 1897 regulation changes. A Board of Generals was convened in 1916 to review every award of the Medal of Honor to date. The Board was headed by General Nelson Miles, a Civil War and Indian Wars veteran, and himself a Medal of Honor recipient. He and his fellow generals examined every record. To keep the deliberations fair and impartial, each file was identified not by

---

[4] On the same day, President Clinton also awarded the much-delayed MOH for President Theodore Roosevelt for his actions at San Juan Hill during the Spanish-American War.

name but a number. The panel published their conclusions on February 5th, 1917. The Board rescinded the 864 medals of the 27th Maine; the awards made to all twenty-nine members of President Lincoln's funeral guard; the Medals for six civilians (who were denied eligibility because they were not members of the military); and, they issued retractions in twelve other cases where the actions underlying the original awards were deemed not to have measured up.[5] The Board's recommendations became known as "The Great Purge."

Interestingly, of the six civilians stripped of their medals, five were Indian scouts, including Buffalo Bill Cody. The Board could not and did not deny their courage; just their eligibility: They were civilians. The sixth award rescinded had originally belonged to Dr. Mary Walker, the only woman to have (so far) been awarded a Medal of Honor. She was singled out for her contributions during the Civil War by Generals William Tecumseh Sherman and George Thomas. There was certainly no doubt that Dr. Walker had served courageously and far above the call of duty. She had even been a prisoner of war for several months, enduring great hardships during her captivity. The problem was this: Dr. Walker, as a Contract Surgeon for the Union Army, was, like the Indian scouts, officially a civilian. Also against her candidacy was that, as a woman, she was ineligible to enlist or be commissioned under laws then extant.

Dr. Walker refused to return her Medal of Honor often saying, "Let 'em come and try and take it." (no-one ever attempted to do so). She wore it defiantly and proudly, every day, until she died in 1919. She and her cause were never

---

[5] Including one Union officer who simply requested one "as a remembrance,"—and got it!

forgotten by her admirers, and President Jimmy Carter restored her Medal of Honor in 1977. Later, in 1989, the five medals taken back from Buffalo Bill and the other Indian scouts were reinstated by President George H. W. Bush.

The "modern era" for the Medal of Honor begins with the Act of 9 July, 1918. Additional stipulations were added to the 1917 requirements:

- Recommendations for award of the Medal of Honor must be made within two years of the actual incident, and bestowed within three.
- From 1918 onward, the Medal of Honor would sit on top of a "Pyramid of Honor." Lesser awards for individual valor were created. Some of these new awards were the Distinguished Service Cross, Navy Cross, and Silver Star.
- From 1918 forward, an individual could only be awarded one Medal of Honor. Prior to 1918, there had been nineteen times when an individual had been awarded two Medals of Honor (but never three or more). One of these men was Tom Custer, younger brother of Lieutenant Colonel George Armstrong Custer.

The first Medal of Honor of WWII was actually earned moments before Japanese bombs started dropping on Pearl Harbor, when Navy Lieutenant John Finn valiantly defended the airfield at Kaneohe, Hawaii, from attack by the first wave of Japanese fliers. [Lieutenant Finn passed away, at age 90, in May, 2010.] The first, and so far only, Medal of Honor earned by a member of the United States Coast Guard was presented posthumously to the family of Petty Officer Douglas Munro, a hero of Guadalcanal, in 1942.

Four hundred seventy-three men merited the Medal of Honor for WWII—only three of them are still alive. One hundred forty-six men were awarded the Medal of Honor for Korea, five are still living; 263 for Vietnam, with 49 men still alive; two posthumous awards for Somalia; 17 awards for Afghanistan with 13 still with us; and six for Iraq, all deceased but one.

The Veteran's Administration provides a pension of $1367 per month to living holders of the Medal of Honor, not that it has ever been about the money. Internment in Arlington National Cemetery is guaranteed, and children of honorees are automatically eligible for matriculation at a service academy of their choice.

The Civil War Era[6]
Chapter 2: First Lieutenant Wilmon W. Blackmar, 1st West Virginia Cavalry

Harvard Affiliation: Law School, JD 1868

Wilmon Blackmar as President, Grand Army of the Republic-1904

On April 1, 1865, with the Civil War in its final days, a 23-year old First Lieutenant in the 1st West Virginia Cavalry, Wilmon W. Blackmar, sat astride his horse at the far left of the Union line near Five Forks, Virginia. His regimental commander was nearby, but Blackmar was not sure exactly where he was. What Blackmar did know was that the

---

[6] Medal of Honor recipients are listed alphabetically in each era.

Confederate forces of Gen. Richard "Baldy" Ewell were squarely in front of him and his men, behind a narrow ditch, and seemed to be ripe for an attack.

Blackmar called for his color bearer to join him in a charge, leaping over the ditch, rallying the cavalry to follow. Before he and the color bearer could move, Blackmar felt a strong hand unexpectedly grip his shoulder. He turned in his saddle to face none other than Major General George Armstrong Custer, his brigade commander. Custer said to Blackmar, "You take the colors and make the charge. The men will follow."

Blackmar did not hesitate. He rode over to the color bearer, grabbed the flag, and bolted, leaping his steed across the ditch and toward the stunned Confederates. The cavalry, as Custer predicted, followed Blackmar's lead. A few of the hungry, tired Rebels fired, but most threw down their weapons or turned and ran. It was a complete and instantaneous victory with no Union casualties.

As hundreds of Confederate prisoners were being rounded up, Gen. Custer once again caught up with Blackmar. He said, "That was fine work, Captain," to which Blackmar replied, "But sir, I am only a Lieutenant." Custer smiled and informed him, "Not any longer. You are hereby promoted Captain on the field."

For his heroic charge at the Battle of Five Forks, Brevet Captain Wilmon Blackmar would receive the Medal of Honor. Like some of his era, the actual award was slow in coming. He did not receive the Medal, in fact, until 1897 when a petition submitted on his behalf finally wound its way through the War Department and was approved by President McKinley's Secretary of War, Russell Alger.

By the time he received his Medal, Blackmar, born July 25, 1841, had led a full and interesting life. At the beginning of the Civil War he had been a 19-year old student at Exeter, prepping for college. His father was a clergyman in Pennsylvania, where Wilmon had been born. His mother was a devoted preacher's wife and homemaker. Blackmar came home from Exeter and enlisted in the 15th Pennsylvania Cavalry in August, 1862. He worked his way through every enlisted rank, right up to First Sergeant. He fought in a number of the major battles of the Civil War (Antietam and Chickamauga, among others) and somehow never received a scratch. He did, though, like hundreds of thousands of his peers, suffer from debilitating disease, in his case typhoid, which struck him down for seven weeks in 1863.

Finally, in March of 1864, he was elevated to the officer ranks and commissioned a 2nd Lieutenant in the 1st West Virginia Cavalry. He spent most of the balance of the war on the staff of whichever general commanded his division. Promoted to 1st Lieutenant in early 1865, he was then an aide to Brigadier General Henry Capehart, but technically still a member of the 1st West Virginia at the time of the Five Forks battle.

After the war concluded, Blackmar enrolled in Harvard Law School, from whence he graduated in 1868. He also joined the Grand Army of the Republic, and was a member of that organization for thirty-seven years, steadily rising through its ranks.

Electing to stay in Massachusetts after law school, he became a partner in a prominent Boston law firm. In 1873 he was appointed Judge Advocate General of Massachusetts with the rank of Brigadier General.

Even with his self-made fortune, prominent status in Boston legal circles, a beautiful estate in Hingham, Massachusetts, and his exalted rank, he most closely associated with the common soldier. He had, after all, spent most of his wartime career in the ranks and served on the front lines with the men who bore the war on their backs and carried it in their souls.

There is an amusing story about the young lieutenant of cavalry that should be told: In mid 1864, just before the beginning of the Petersburg Campaign, as the cavalry of both sides ranged across the landscape, raiding each other's supplies, Confederate General Fitzhugh Lee's cavalry captured several wagons in General Custer's baggage train. Custer was hit particularly hard as the Rebels picked him clean: they rode off with all his spare uniforms, most of his personal grooming items—including his toothbrush—and a packet of love letters that his wife Libbie had sent to him.

The correspondence between George and Libbie, as history has shown, was often poetic and extremely loving; plus, it could, from time to time, even border on the pre-Victorian erotic. A trove of passionate love letters captured by the Rebels and passed around in a ribald fashion weighed heavily on Libbie's mind.

In early 1865, near the Union lines at Petersburg, Lt. Blackmar's men had taken a young Confederate prisoner. The man had only just gotten back on duty after a long period of convalescence for sickness. Blackmar had taken pity on the boy because he was still weak and had given him food, some warm clothes, and had let him ride his horse instead of slogging back to the Union lines on foot. For these great kindnesses, the soldier, who seemed to know that Blackmar was a big admirer of Custer, told his benefactor that he knew where Custer's missing love letters were being held. Apparently, as Libbie feared, they were being handed around and read with great amusement.

Using a clever ruse and some disguises, the Confederate and Blackmar snuck into the town, met up with the current holder of the purloined packet, pretended to be interested in reading them, then snatched the letters and rode pell-mell back to the Union lines.

With great glee, Blackmar raced to Custer's tent, asked to see the General and presented the lost letters to their rightful owner. Blackmar related that, "He took them making no answer, but laughing and dancing around the (tent)."

Blackmar, as mentioned, spent many years after the war diligently engaged in activities supporting the Grand Army of the Republic. In 1904, he was elected its National President. Sadly, his tenure was all too short: on the way to the 1905 National Convention, he was stricken, in Boise, Idaho, with a fatal inflammation of the kidneys.

His remains were returned to Massachusetts where the old warrior's body was honored by lying in state at the Massachusetts State Capitol before final burial in Dorchester.

Citation:

"The President of the United States of America, in the name of Congress, takes pleasure in presenting the Medal of Honor to Lieutenant Wilmon Whilldin Blackmar, United States Army, for extraordinary heroism on 1 April 1865, while serving with Company H, 1st West Virginia Cavalry, in action at Five Forks, Virginia. At a critical stage of the battle,

without orders, Lieutenant Blackmar led a successful advance upon the enemy."

Was Custer's remark to Blackmar an order--or just a "suggestion?"

Chapter 3: Surgeon (Major) Richard J. Curran, 33rd New York Volunteer Infantry

Harvard Affiliation: Medical School, MD 1859

Dr. Richard Curran, as Mayor, Rochester, NY 1892

During the great Irish Diaspora of the mid-19th century, millions emigrated from the "old sod" to all parts of the globe, but the vast majority went to England, Scotland, Australia, Canada, and the United States. The family of Richard Curran, who was born in Carrahill, County Clare, on January 13th, 1838, was part of this vast migration. His parents, Richard and Catharine, brought young Richard and his siblings to settle in Seneca Falls, New York in 1850.

By several accounts Richard was a bright and industrious young man. He was enrolled in Seneca Falls

Academy and when he graduated, at age 16, he went to work at the drugstore of Mr. J. E. Clark.

His efficient work at the pharmacy brought him to the attention of two local doctors, who convinced him to apprentice in their offices. Two years later, both doctors sponsored him for Harvard Medical School. He graduated, at age 21, in 1859. Additional post-graduate work followed under the guidance of the eminent Harvard physician Dr. Oliver Wendell Holmes, Sr., (father of the future Supreme Court Justice). Dr. Curran returned to Seneca Falls, his medical education complete, just in time to witness the advent of the Civil War.

Like many men his age he rallied to the flag, enlisting on May 22nd, 1861, in Company K, the 33rd New York Regiment. His expertise in medicine did not keep him in the ranks of the infantry for long, however. In October, he was promoted to Hospital Steward, a position roughly equal to a senior sergeant's rank. By August 1862 he was promoted again, to Assistant Surgeon, an officer's billet that was equivalent to a First Lieutenant.

Less than a month later, the 33rd New York found itself thrown into the Civil War battle that became known as "the single bloodiest day in American history:" It was September 17th, 1862, the Battle of Antietam. The fight came on fast, and it rapidly became frenzied and ferocious. At the end of the day, a total of 22,717 Americans, from both sides, were casualties. In Curran's brigade, 313 men were killed or wounded. The 33rd alone lost six killed and thirty-eight wounded.

For Dr. Curran, it was an especially hellacious day. Due to a quirk of logistics and timing, he was the only medical officer near the front lines of the 3rd Brigade. The rest of the medical team, including all the ambulances, orderlies, and other surgeons, were in the rear trying to work their way forward.

The 33rd and the other regiments nearby had been charging back and forth across a shallow valley all day, neither side achieving a clear advantage. The result of all the back-and-forth action was the creation of hundreds of casualties in blue and butternut strewn across the open ground between the lines.

Dr. Curran organized small groups of volunteers to rush into the carnage and evacuate the wounded from both armies. He, himself, dashed onto the field numerous times to treat the afflicted and helped get many of them back to his makeshift field hospital. The "hospital" wasn't much: It consisted of bales of hay stacked high enough to cordon off the most seriously wounded and provide some minimal shelter from the flying lead. Dr. Curran constantly worried about the hay catching fire, but as treacherous as it was, it was the best he could do given the circumstances. The officers and men urged him, on numerous occasions, to go to the rear, to safety, and come back when the battle ceased. He consistently refused.

Dr. Curran labored well into the night and long after the firing halted. It was apparent to his regimental and brigade commanders that he and his orderlies had saved dozens, perhaps hundreds, of lives with their courage and timely ministrations. He was prominently mentioned in the brigade after action report, which cited him for his coolness and bravery under fire.

The 33rd was a two-year regiment, so when its term of obligated service was over, in June of 1863, the regiment mustered out. The war, of course, was not over, and Dr. Curran felt he was still needed so he immediately signed on as Assistant Surgeon of the 6th New York Cavalry. When that regiment mustered out, in September 1864, he joined the 9th New York Cavalry and was promoted to Surgeon (a Major's rank). He remained with the 9th until the war's end and was a witness to Lee's surrender at Appomattox.

Beginning shortly after the Battle of Antietam, a number of Dr. Curran's friends and fellow regimental veterans began to urge him to apply for the Medal of Honor. If not awarded outright or recommended immediately, the Medal could be requested by petition. Dr. Curran steadfastly refused, saying that he had only done his duty, nothing more, and there the matter would rest, as far as Dr. Curran was concerned.

Dr. Curran returned to Seneca Falls, married Mary Rogers, had a daughter, and then moved to Rochester, New York. In Rochester, he and an old friend from the 6th New York started what became a very successful pharmacy. He also delved into the political life of "The Flour City" (so-named because the Erie Canal had made Rochester the number-one city in America in the production of milled flour.)

Dr. Curran served as the city's School Commissioner in 1876-77; Parks Commissioner from 1878-79; and was elected to the State Legislature in 1891. He did not serve out his term, however, because the political machine in Rochester wanted him back, this time as Mayor. He was elected by an overwhelming margin in 1892, ultimately serving two terms (1892-1896).

Sadly, his wife Mary died suddenly in 1875. He remarried in 1881 to Katie Whelan, with whom he had four more children.

The Curran Administration in Rochester City Hall was a relatively quiet one. The only real controversy was a movement to do away with the long-standing city Executive Board, a group of prominent local gentlemen who acted more like a board of directors for the city than a city council. They basically controlled everything, including the awarding of city contracts.

The challenge to the stranglehold of the Executive Board was successful and it resulted in the Mayor's office becoming much more powerful. This, in turn, attracted the attention of men who were more ambitious than Dr. Curran. He stepped aside when his second term as Mayor was complete, and happily returned to his pharmacy.

In 1898, Curran either had a change of heart or finally bowed to the urgings of his friends and family. Curran sent a respectful letter to the Secretary of War, Russell Alger, requesting that he be awarded the Medal of Honor. His humble missive reads, in part:

"For some time many of my army friends who knew of my perilous position in this battle (Antietam)…have urged me to apply for the Medal of Honor as they believed me entitled to it. I have hesitated…largely because it might be urged that the position for a medical officer during a battle was in the rear and in a place of safety…but in answer I want to say, that my regiment was ordered into this fight immediately on arriving on the battlefield in the absence of orders and with the best intentions I followed and happily in no other position could I have rendered equally as good service, for I am confident that by my action many lives were saved."

President McKinley apparently agreed and directed that Dr. Curran be awarded the MOH. After Dr. Curran received his Medal of Honor he displayed it proudly. He became a member of the Medal of Honor Legion, joined the Marshall Post of the Grand Army of the Republic, and served for a number of years as a director of the Oxford (New York) Soldier's Home.

A history of the City of Rochester was published in 1902 and in it there is a telling comment about the public perception of Dr. Curran:

"At all times and under all circumstances he has been found true to every trust reposed in him, whether public or private, and over his life record there falls no shadow of wrong or suspicion of evil." [7]

The good doctor and faithful old soldier lived until June 1915, when he passed away at his home, in his own bed, at the age of 77.

Citation:

"At Antietam, Md., September 17, 1862, this officer, then Assistant Surgeon, 33rd New York Volunteers, and in charge of the Field Hospital of the 3rd Brigade, 2nd Division, 6th Army Corps, when urged by some of his comrades to remain in a place of safety in rear as was his privilege, disregarded these requests and voluntarily exposed himself to very great danger by going to the fighting line, there succoring the wounded and helpless and conducting them to

---

[7] The Biographical Record of the City of Rochester and Monroe County, New York; New York & Chicago, S.J. Clarke Publishing Co., 1902, pp. 145-146.

the Field Hospital. He remained with the wounded throughout the battle at the Hospital, which was also within the range of the enemy's fire. The Brigade Commander, in his official report of the battle, particularly commends Assistant Surgeon Curran for his services and example."

Chapter 4: Major General Manning Ferguson Force, 1st Brigade, 3rd Division, XVII Corps

Harvard Affiliation: AB, 1845; JD 1848

Brig. Gen. Force, 1864

July 22, 1864, was a sweltering hot day in Georgia. Thirty-nine year-old Brigadier General Manning Force was trying to take advantage of a slight breeze as he stood atop Bald Hill, overlooking the soon-to-be ravaged city of Atlanta. Force commanded the 1st Brigade of Leggett's Division in the massive Union Army of Major General William Tecumseh Sherman. General Force and his men had fought and clawed their way to the top of the hill the day before, pushing off a determined Confederate defense. They commanded the heights and were desperately trying to bring up artillery so that the City of Atlanta, lying helplessly below, could be blasted into submission.

As the Union soldiers worked to consolidate their positions, the dispossessed Confederates, led by General John Bell Hood in person, made a sudden and sweeping counter-attack against General Leggett's command. The Rebels swarmed up the slope of Bald Hill intending to retake their former works.

General Force and his men bent to the task and managed to stem the tide and hold their ground. Force stood bravely at the front of his men, stalwartly directing the defense. As he did so, an enemy Minie ball smashed into his face just below his left eye, plowed through the soft palate and exited his skull just behind the right eye. The wound was believed to be fatal and Force was carried off the field to die.

Though grievously scarred and critically wounded, the General somehow managed to survive. He even returned to duty just three months later. For his valor at Bald Hill, renamed Leggett's Hill, Force was brevetted to Major General and decorated with the Medal of Honor (although it was not bestowed until much later, in 1892).

Manning Force was born in Washington, DC, on December 17th, 1824. His father, Peter, was a prominent printer and editor of the *National Journal*. The elder Force was a staunch supporter of John Quincy Adams and served two terms as Mayor of Washington, DC (1836 to 1840). Perhaps his greatest contribution to history, however, was his campaign to establish a national library. Peter had amassed a truly significant collection of documents from the American

Revolution, including a number of very rare pamphlets and tracts written by several of the Founding Fathers. Peter Force lived long enough (1868) to see the establishment of his hoped-for repository. The Congress purchased Force's own collection in 1867 for $100,000 and that collection was the core of what ultimately became the Library of Congress.

Perhaps due to the influence of the Adams family, young Manning was sent off to Harvard. He graduated with the Class of 1845, immediately enrolled in Harvard Law School, and graduated from there as well in 1848. His first offer of employment was obtained from a law firm in Cincinnati. He accepted and moved to Ohio, where he would reside for the rest of his life. He passed the Ohio bar in 1850 and formed a law practice with two partners.

He joined the Literary Club of Cincinnati, a group of like-minded men who would have a profound impact on Manning Force. Among the members were Lincoln's eventual Secretary of the Treasury, Salmon P. Chase; the Civil War General John Pope; and, future President Rutherford B. Hayes. Force's friendship with Hayes was particularly close and the two men would remain good friends for the rest of their days.

The Literary Club sponsored a military company called the Burnet Rifles and it was due to Force's membership in this organization that he received an appointment as a major in the 20th Ohio Volunteer Infantry in August 1861. When the Colonel of the 20th was tapped to direct the building of the defenses around Cincinnati in September, Force was moved up to Lieutenant Colonel and placed in temporary command of the 20th.

Force had very limited military experience, but he was a quick study. He was a strict disciplinarian but well-liked for the care and concern he showed toward his men. The recruits responded to his leadership, and the 20th became known throughout the Army of the Tennessee as a tough and dependable regiment.

The regiment's first action didn't come until February 1862, when the 20th got bloodied but held firm at Fort Donelson. Two months later, at Shiloh, Force had to take command of the regiment when his colonel became ill. In May, Force was given permanent command—and promoted to colonel.

Force and the 20th Ohio were thrust into national prominence when they held off Nathan Bedford Forrest's cavalry in a gallant defense of the Union line at Bolivar, Tennessee, in August 1862. At Corinth and Vicksburg, the 20th was in the forefront again. Force received special recognition for his actions at the Battle of Raymond, in May 1863, when he threw his regiment forward to stymie a spirited Confederate attack. In August 1863, Force was promoted to brigadier general and given command of the 1st Brigade of Leggett's Division of the 17th Corps. It had been a rapid rise to general for a lawyer with little military background.

After his wounding at Atlanta, General Force recuperated at home until October. On his return to duty, Sherman had him brevetted to major general and gave him command of the 3rd Division. He marched his men with Sherman to the sea, then turned his troops north, through the Carolinas. After the war's end, General Force was made military governor of Mississippi. In January 1866, he turned down a Colonel's commission in the Regular Army to return home to Cincinnati and his law practice.

Later in 1866, he was elected judge of the Hamilton County Courts, a position he held until 1875. He married in 1874 (at age 50) to Frances Horton, sister-in-law to Major General John Pope—his old friend from the Literary Club. He and Frances had one son, Horton, born in 1878.

Force ran for Congress in 1876, losing narrowly, but his friend, Rutherford Hayes, was elected to the White House. The new President offered Force the job of Personal Presidential Secretary. Force turned it down deeming the job "insufficiently prestigious" for a man of his skills and accomplishments.

In 1877 Force became a professor of law at Cincinnati Law School and was elected judge of the Superior Court of Cincinnati. He remained on the bench until 1887 when overwork and stress caused him to have a nervous breakdown.

Hayes (by then out of office) took Force and his family into his own home and sent them all on a month-long trip to Europe, at his expense. The vacation got Force on the road to recovery. After his return, his friend Hayes stepped in again and got Force appointed to the post of Commandant of the Ohio Soldier's Home in Sandusky, Ohio. This was a job much to Force's liking and perfectly suited to his temperament. He stayed on as commandant, exercising the same care and concern he had once shown for his former troops, until he passed away peacefully on May 8, 1899.

Citation:

"Charged upon the enemy's works, and after their capture defended his position against assaults of the enemy until he was severely wounded."

Chapter 5: Lieutenant Colonel Henry Shippen Huidekoper, 150th Pennsylvania Infantry, US Volunteers

Harvard Affiliation: AB, 1862; AM, 1872

Lt. Col. Huidekoper, 1863

The Battle of Gettysburg has assumed a sacred place in the history of American conflict. Over three harrowing days of combat, from July 1 to July 3, 1863, the ultimate fate of two nations was decided. The North, with its powerful but erratically led armies, had stumbled from one engagement to another over the course of nearly three years of hard fighting. Rarely had the Union won a significant contest—until Gettysburg.

Conversely, the opposing armies of the South had been well-handled, even with their rag-tag uniforms, inferior equipment and meager provisions. They had been imbued with a confidence that allowed them to believe they could never be "whipped"--until Gettysburg. Those three sweltering days in July reversed everything for General Robert E. Lee and his men. The crushing rebuff of Pickett's Charge, on July 3rd, became known as "the high water mark of the Confederacy," and rightfully so. Indeed, as the shattered remains of Pickett's Division smashed into the stone wall atop Cemetery Ridge, the very center of the Union lines, it seemed as if the tidal wave of Southern arms reached its maximum flow. When the tattered remnants of Pickett's brigades ebbed back to where they had started, everything was different.

After Gettysburg, the Union forces in the eastern theater gained confidence, and momentum. They began to push the Confederates harder and all across the map. From July 3 on, the Confederate strategy was about the defensive, and achieving stalemate. It was no longer about capturing Washington and winning the war. The goal became one of suing for peace. It was a profound difference on many levels, thanks mostly to the events at Gettysburg.

Sixty-four men were decorated with the MOH for their actions at Gettysburg. The soldier who probably gained the most fame from his MOH at Gettysburg was Col. (later Major General) Joshua Lawrence Chamberlain. He was the commander of the 20th Maine, an under-strength regiment of roughly 350 men who, solely by chance, ended up as the very last band of soldiers anchoring the far left of the Union lines.

The Maine men were stationed on a low knoll called Little Round Top. There was not another Union soldier beyond their left flank. If the Confederates could get around the 20th, they would be free to roll up and crush the entire Union line. Should they have accomplished that, the results of the battle would have been entirely different.

The Confederates did not succeed, but it wasn't for lack of trying. Lt. Gen. "Pete" Longstreet sent the 16th Alabama smashing into the 20th Maine, trying to overwhelm and get around the defiant Maine men. Using a textbook maneuver he had recently read in a tactics manual, Chamberlain "refused his line;" that is, he bent a large part of it backwards to block the Rebel advance. When the onslaught stalled, as it did in the face of the 20th's intensive fire, Chamberlain then used his bent-back line like a huge barn door and ordered the line to swing on its "hinges" and slam the door shut on the Alabamians.

Chamberlain and his men saved the Union lines from disaster. Rising to general rank, suffering several wounds, Chamberlain went on to even more glory and success: he received the surrender of Lee's army at Appomattox; became President of Bowdoin College; and served three terms as Governor of Maine.

Before Chamberlain and his men performed their heroics on the left, far across the battlefield, on the right, on July 1, another brave officer held steadfast for his country, suffering a grievous wound for his valor but eventually a MOH.

Lt. Col. Henry Shippen Huidekoper, one year out from graduation with Harvard's Class of 1862, found himself, on the morning of July 1, suddenly in command of the 150th Pennsylvania Infantry. He and his men were encamped near the stone-walled McPherson barn--a proud landmark of the battle that still stands today. The 24-year old Philadelphian had been in the Army less than a year, had barely seen any combat, then found himself on one of the greatest stages of the war, about to play a crucial part.

The Class of 1862 had a tumultuous four years at Harvard College. The outbreak of the Civil War and the events leading up to it had plunged many college campuses into fierce debates about slavery, states' rights, emancipation, and secession. Harvard was no exception. Many prominent southern families, especially alumni, had, for generations, sent their sons to Harvard. When the war began many young southern gentlemen were still enrolled. Schisms between the northern students and the "southrons" were wide. Most of the faculty took up the cause of the Union and abolition. Classes were disrupted with impromptu shouting matches. Fisticuffs were not uncommon. There were food fights in the dining halls.

By the spring of 1862, nearly all the students with enduring southern ties had "gone south." Ultimately, 257 Harvard alumni would serve the Confederacy and 64 of these alumni would die during the war, 52 of them killed in action.

Brigadier General Ben Hardin Helm, CSA, Class of 1853, who was killed at Chickamauga, was Mary Todd Lincoln's brother. Captain Robert Hitt, CSA, Class of 1855, was shot dead at the Battle of Prairie Grove in December, 1862, while his brother, Union Captain S. N. Hitt, fired on the Rebels from across the field--a true embodiment of the classic Civil War descriptor of "brother against brother."

A young Confederate sergeant from the Class of 1864, with the ironic name of George Washington died. He was the great grandson of the first president's younger brother James.

Hundreds of Harvard alumni flocked to the Union banner. There were even enough Harvard volunteers from Massachusetts to form the so-called "Harvard Regiment," the 20th Massachusetts Infantry. Captain Oliver Wendell Holmes, Jr., Class of 1861, was a member (wounded in action) as was Colonel Paul Revere, Class of 1852, grandson of the famous "midnight rider" (died of wounds received at Gettysburg, July 4, 1863).

Henry Huidekoper was born in Meadville, Pennsylvania on July 17, 1839. His parents were prosperous and came from solid banking and mercantile families. Henry was tempted several times to drop out of college as the Civil War began, but he stayed the course and graduated with his class. Immediately after he received his diploma he went back home to Philadelphia and used his family's connections with the Governor to obtain a commission as a captain in the newly organized 150th Pennsylvania.

Although Henry's military training had been nil prior to his commissioning, he proved to be a quick study. He was a good and steady officer, well liked by the men. By September, 1862, he had moved up to lieutenant colonel, effectively second-in-command of the regiment.

The 150th was part of the (soon to be famous) Bucktail Brigade, consisting of the 143rd, 149th, and 150th regiments. In an army which was mostly a sea of blue uniforms, none more distinct than another, the brigade adopted a fashion of affixing a deer's tail to their hatbands, thus becoming "The Pennsylvania Bucktails." This bravado would, of course, have to be backed up by performance, and when called upon, the brigade would more than prove its worth.

The 150th was ordered into the field for the first time in February, 1863. As part of the new First Army Corp their initial assignment was to guard the nation's capitol. In April, the 150th was re-assigned to the 2nd Brigade, 3rd Division, Army of the Potomac. They were sent to a provincial backwater crossroads named Chancellorsville. This was where General Lee famously crushed Gen. "Fighting Joe" Hooker, but lost his most talented subordinate, Lt. Gen. Thomas "Stonewall" Jackson, shot down mistakenly by his own men.

The 150th was mostly in reserve at Chancellorsville, but they did see some rearguard action as the Union army fled. They suffered their first casualties, but not many.

Hooker was yanked from his post as the Union forces slunk away. Maj. Gen. George Gordon Meade, who did not want the job, was placed in command. The army licked its wounds and started a march toward central Pennsylvania as intelligence indicated Lee was aiming to capture Harrisburg, the capitol.

Fate would cause the two giant forces of Lee and Meade to stumble into each other at the tiny crossroads town of Gettysburg.

On June 30, Lt. Col. Huidekoper and the 150th were tramping down the Chambersburg Pike (today's US Route 30) along with tens of thousands of Union soldiers. The Bucktail Brigade was in the lead, a position of honor among the column. The sun shone down on the men from a cloudless sky. The temperature was in the mid-seventies; not unbearable for marching unless, like nearly all the men, one was wearing the heavy blue serge wool standard uniform and carrying, on average, about 60 pounds of food, water, ammunition, equipment, and a rifle. Dust from the horses, men, and the dry dirt road swirled skyward. The signs of this army's movements could be seen from ten miles away.

Every man knew they were headed into another battle: It was only a matter of where and when, but all knew it would be soon. The electricity of anticipation shot through the long column. Even the horses seemed nervous.

Lt. Col. Huidekoper, not normally a superstitious man, had a premonition he could not shake, the result of his last night's dreams. He saw himself being wounded in the coming battle, and not having the means to stop his bleeding. He asked his orderly to make a tourniquet for him, which the man did. Huidekoper hurriedly stuffed it in his tunic.

Late in the afternoon, the column stopped for the day. The 150th was ordered to go into camp, in a field, near McPherson's barn, a half mile west of Gettysburg.

The following morning, just after 8:00 AM, Union pickets from the 8th Illinois Cavalry came upon Rebel pickets from Gen. Henry Heth's division. Heth and his men had been pushing ahead of Lee's main body, heading to the town of Gettysburg, where they hoped to find a rumored cache of shoes (it was not true). Heth was under strict orders from Lee that if he encountered Union forces he was not to bring on a full engagement: he was to halt and report back to Lee.

Heth was either overcome by the moment or decided to disobey Lee's instructions. He ordered his men to charge ahead. After brushing back the Union cavalry pickets, Heth's division came upon Brig. Gen. John Buford's entire cavalry regiment. Buford, a seasoned West Pointer of exceptional experience and skill, a veteran of the Regular Army, instantly knew what he had to do: delay.

Buford and his men fell back slowly, away from the numerically superior Confederates. Buford then executed one of the most fortuitous Union moves of the battle: he placed his men squarely atop Seminary Ridge, overlooking the Rebels coming on from below. This gave Buford a commanding view, the ability to shoot down on his attackers, and it secured a position of great strategic value. It also gave him the ability to buy time until reinforcements and the big guns came rolling up behind him.

The battle soon widened as more and more units from both sides came up and pitched in. The 32nd North Carolina came rushing forward and found itself squarely in front of the 150th Pennsylvania.

As firing commenced, the brigade commander, Col. Roy Stone, was immediately shot from his saddle. Brigade command transferred to the senior regimental colonel who happened to be Col. Langhorne Wister, commander of the 150th. These moves placed command of the 150th in the hands of Lt. Col. Huidekoper.

The commander of the 32nd North Carolina ordered an advance. Huidekoper, waving his sword over his head, steadied his men and made sure they were in a solid double-rank line facing the enemy, the front rank kneeling, the rear rank standing. When all was to his satisfaction, he ordered his men to fire in unison.

The effect on the Carolinians was staggering as dozens of men went down at once. Their advance was halted, but not their determination. The survivors closed ranks, un-shouldered their rifles, and unleashed a punishing volley of their own, directly into the 150th.

When the smoke cleared both lines were reeling. Every officer in the 150th, except for Huidekoper, was wounded or dead. The moment hung on a thread. Huidekoper did not hesitate. Raising his sword once more he ordered another volley, then a bayonet charge.

The remaining men of the 150th went forward with a shout. The 32nd North Carolina hesitated, but finally broke and headed back down the road. The 150th had held--and prevailed. They had done their duty that day with great courage and determination, and did so under the leadership of their valiant lieutenant colonel.

As the men shouted in celebration, some noticed their commander was not with them. Then a senior sergeant spotted the colonel kneeling in the grass a few yards behind the line. He was obviously wounded. Indeed, he was: a ball had grazed his right thigh. It was a bloody wound, but minor. Of more concern was the .52 caliber Minie ball that had struck Huidekoper's right arm, just below the elbow.

The standard ball, used by both sides, was a spherical shot of considerable size. When it struck the human body it did not simply penetrate flesh: the Minie ball ripped through flesh and if it struck bones, it often shattered them into splinters. Even an arm wound like Huidekoper's could prove fatal, given the medical standards of the day--which were not high.

Huidekoper's premonition had proven accurate. He remembered the tourniquet tucked in his tunic and took it out right away. His men applied it, and the bleeding slowed.

The brave colonel, although in excruciating pain, refused to leave the field. He would not seek aid while the command was still in danger. Finally, an hour later, the Reserves came up and he was relieved of duty, free to find a surgeon.

The situation all across the field of battle was chaotic, but Huidekoper was told that a field hospital had been set up in the village. Still bleeding and wracked with pain, he somehow managed to walk the half mile to downtown Gettysburg. The Confederates were then in control of the town, but there was, indeed, a hospital set up in and around the church, and it was treating men from both sides.

A harried Union surgeon examined Huidekoper and gave him the bad news: his right arm would have to go, or he would die. After a quick swig of whisky, the young colonel was lashed to a table and the surgeon took off his right arm, in three quick strokes of his bone saw, just above the elbow,.

After bandaging, the dazed Huidekoper was told to find a spot to lie down and rest. He found a space to stretch out in the church gallery, near the bell tower.

Quite by chance, Confederate Lt. Gen. Richard "Old Baldy" Ewell and his staff were standing nearby observing the fighting swirling around the village.

Huidekoper heard Ewell boast to his subordinates, "Well, we've licked the Yankees now!"

Huidekoper struggled to his feet. Holding his empty right sleeve with his left arm, he angrily shouted at Ewell, "Damn you, sir, we're not done yet!"

Startled, Ewell simply stared at the maimed and blood stained young colonel, and kept his counsel. The knot of Confederates then moved off, away from the church.

Huidekoper remained at the makeshift hospital until the Union re-took the village on July 3. His wounds forced him from active duty for two months; then, in September, he was back with the 150th. He was promoted to full colonel and given official command of the regiment.

The rigors of campaigning continued to sap his strength, however, and he finally had to give up his command. He resigned his commission in early 1864 and returned home. He had just turned 25.

Many of Huidekoper's peers said that his gallant stand at McPherson's Barn had been one of the turning points of the battle. His leadership and bravery had been well documented in after action reports, but that was the sum total of the recognition--until a group of Huidekoper's friends, in 1905, were successful in lobbying for a MOH for the 66 year old veteran.

By the time Huidekoper finally received his MOH he had, between the end of the Civil War and 1905, been Major General in charge of the Pennsylvania National Guard, Postmaster General of Philadelphia, an early executive of the Bell Telephone Company, and an Overseer of Harvard College. He had also earned a Master's degree from Harvard in 1872.

Huidekoper lived a long and prosperous life, full of honors and achievements before passing away in 1918 at age 79. Even if most Americans have not heard of him, every one of us has been affected by him. It was Postmaster Henry Huidekoper who, in the 1880s, instituted the standard one-ounce measure for mailing a letter via the Postal Service--a standard that is still in effect today.

Citation:

"While engaged in repelling an attack of the enemy, received a severe wound of the right arm, but instead of retiring remained at the front in command of the regiment."

Chapter 6: Captain Henry W. Lawton, 30th Indiana Infantry, US Volunteers

Harvard Affiliation: Law School, 1866

Maj. Gen. Lawton 1898

Henry Lawton has been largely forgotten in today's popular military lore, but in the latter half of the 19th century he was a larger-than-life figure, both literally and figuratively. He was six-foot-five and never much less than 250 pounds; so he towered over most men of his day. His exploits and exotic postings were frequently featured in popular periodicals and national newspapers. There were good reasons for his fame: he was a Medal of Honor recipient for his courage in the Civil

War; legendary Indian fighter; captor of Geronimo; led the first US troops ashore in Cuba during the Spanish-American War; and, a popular General with both the Americans and the Filipinos during the Philippine Insurrection (1899-1902).

Most often seen with a thick, bushy, mustache, "Long Hank" as he was popularly known, cut quite the figure and he placed a very large stamp on the history of the United States Army during his nearly four decades of service.

Henry Lawton was born on March 17th, 1843, in Maumee, Ohio, to George and Catherine Lawton. George was a millwright (skilled mechanic and carpenter) who worked on agricultural machinery. Sadly, Henry's mother died when he was only nine. His father took jobs in a number of locations, so Henry spent a great deal of time, along with his two brothers, in the care of friends and relatives. In 1858, he was living in Fort Wayne, Indiana, and when the Civil War broke out in 1861, he was studying at Methodist Episcopal College.

Henry enlisted right away, as a three-month volunteer, in the 9th Indiana. When the 9th mustered out ninety days later, the war, of course, was still raging and looked like it was going to go on for much longer than most people had predicted; so, In August 1861, Henry signed up again, this time with the newly organized 30th Indiana. He was made, in rapid order, a first sergeant, then a First Lieutenant. After the battle of Shiloh, in April 1862, he was promoted to Captain.

Lawton fought in twenty-two major engagements during the Civil War, a veritable compendium of the war's most sanguine battles including Shiloh, Stone's River, Chickamauga, Iuka, Corinth and the Battle of Atlanta. Amazingly, during four years of hard fighting, Lawton was never wounded—and he was not shy about being in the front lines and in the thick of every fight. He generated an aura of invincibility and he used it as a mantle: It only failed him once, much later in life.

Lawton and the 30th Indiana, in which he served for most of the war, were constantly being mentioned in after action reports, and always positively. Lawton was garnering much recognition for his leadership and bravery but his finest moment in the war undoubtedly came at the gates of Atlanta on August 3rd, 1864.

Leading the 30th's Company A, Lawton was tasked with taking a series of enemy rifle pits in front of his regiment's position. He stormed the trenches with his men and killed or captured all the enemy sharpshooters in that section of the line. If that weren't enough, he and his troops held the same trenches against two stubborn and very determined counter-attacks. It would take another twenty-nine years, but this was the action for which Lawton would be recognized with a Medal of Honor. The Medal was finally bestowed in 1893.

He was promoted, in February of 1865, to Lieutenant Colonel and at the war's end, two months later, brevetted to Colonel, at the tender age of twenty-two.

Lawton decided he wanted to stay in the Army and he lobbied hard for a regular commission, hoping to be made a Captain. He had plenty of influential senior-officer patrons to speak on his behalf; but, in 1865, no one knew what a post-war Army was going to look like except that it would be considerably smaller. There was no certainty whatsoever that Lawton would be accepted and there were thousands of candidates for a few hundred regular commissions.

To hedge his bets, Lawton decided to "read for the law" and joined a Fort Wayne law office in late 1865. At the urging of his employer, he elected to pursue further study of the law at Harvard. He enrolled in Harvard Law School in the summer of 1866. At the same time, as luck would have it, he finally received an offer of a Regular Army commission. Much to his disappointment, it was only a lowly second lieutenant's posting so he decided to stay in law school—at least for the time being.

By the end of his first year at Harvard, his military sponsors were actively urging him to take the commission anyway. It was not likely that any better offer would be forthcoming and he was told if he didn't take what was being offered, it was probably the end of his Army ambitions altogether.

The pull proved to be strong and Lawton decided to take the commission; so, at the end of his first year at Harvard Law, he withdrew, in good academic standing. He would never return to Harvard—or the law.

Second Lieutenant Lawton, Regular Army, was posted in May, 1867, to the 41st Infantry, a so-called "Black Regiment" of African-American soldiers. An unanticipated vacancy in the officer ranks allowed him to be promoted to first lieutenant in July. The 41st was commanded by the legendary Colonel Ranald Mackenzie, who became a friend, confidant and powerful patron.

In 1871, Lawton transferred to the 4th Cavalry, following his mentor Mackenzie. He was promoted to Captain at last and thus began a long, hard, grueling decade-and-a-half of service on the frontier battling Indians, the desert, and the "bottle," the scourge of many a soldier during those difficult times.

Lawton's most glorious exploit during this period was the pursuit and ultimate capture of the mystical Indian leader,

Geronimo. The tale of Lawton's four month long slog, in 1886, through the arroyos and mountains of the Southwest, is an epic story of survival and hardship, patience and persistence, determination and courage. At the end of the trail, with Geronimo in hand, the normally burly Lawton had lost forty pounds and he and his men were reduced to rags for uniforms and stick figures for horses—but they had gotten the job done.

It was during this adventure that Lawton and Leonard Wood became professional associates and very close friends. The ambitious Wood, as the Assistant Surgeon in Lawton's hardy band, would endure all the same hardships as Lawton and his men. As we shall see in relating the tale of Wood, himself, (Chapter 10) this alliance would become a curious and interesting intersection of Harvard men and the Medal of Honor.

Lawton's pursuit of Geronimo became the stuff of legend and led, through additional patronage and connections, to Lawton obtaining a coveted position in the Army Inspector General's Office, promotion to Major; and, shortly hereafter, Lieutenant Colonel. Lawton's star was on the rise.

When the Spanish-American War erupted in 1898, Lawton was given command of the 2nd Division of the 5th Corps and promoted to Brigadier General of Volunteers. He sailed off to Cuba with his men, landing there in June 1898.

Lawton's record in Cuba was mixed. Part of his challenge, despite thirty-seven years of tough soldering and frequent combat, was that he had never led more than 300 troops in battle. As a division commander, he had thousands of troops to direct. He was required to use them effectively, and he had to tackle fluid situations on tricky battlefields.

His most famous exploit in Cuba was the assault on the Spanish positions at El Caney. The Spanish had roughly 630 soldiers, plus artillery, and were entrenched behind fixed positions at the top of a steep hill. Lawton had roughly twelve times that number, but his men were mostly green volunteers and many had been in uniform for only a few weeks.

Lawton failed to reconnoiter the battlefield properly and essentially fell victim to the wide-spread belief among the Americans—far from true—that the Spanish defenders were "soft" and cowardly. The Spanish soldiers were, in fact, well-trained, well-led, generally better armed than the Americans, supremely motivated and; ultimately, very courageous. Lawton went at them as if they were a band of hungry, exhausted Sioux carrying nothing more than bows and arrows, and his hubris cost his division many casualties.

Lawton's superior numbers and the raw jingoism of his untested troops ultimately carried the day; but, it was not a pretty victory. The after-action reports and the generally patriotic press accounts of the battle glossed over many of the inadequacies of Lawton's leadership. In short, he was lucky.

The Cuban campaign was over quickly. The Spanish, brave as they were, simply didn't have the depth to resist the American juggernaut for very long. Lawton was feted as a hero and awarded with the military governorship of Santiago Province.

This assignment proved frustrating for Lawton. His men were succumbing to tropical disease faster than they could be replaced. He was lonely and far from his family. He, himself, contracted malaria. He fell back into an old habit of binge drinking and during one memorable weekend bender, he single-handedly destroyed one of the city's small taverns.

Due to his reputation, his many powerful friends, and his personal relationship with President McKinley, he was quietly recalled to Washington. The Army and the press chalked up his behavior to the effects of "tropical fever." He swore a personal oath to the President, who had been furious at Lawton, that he would stop drinking—a promise that he kept for the rest of his life. Cautiously, he was given probationary command of the 4th Army Corps and a chance to rehabilitate his reputation.

In early 1899, the Philippines erupted. There was a strong independence movement afoot; and, as a legacy of defeating the Spanish the previous year, the Philippines became a headache for the United States. Lawton was dispatched to become part of the Army's mission to subdue the rebels.

From January to December, Lawton and his command, including his old 4th Cavalry, ranged up and down Luzon, pursuing the Philippine rebels. Lawton went at it as he always had: full bore and out in front, leading the troops. His fearlessness—some said his recklessness—was part of his legend. His belief in his imperviousness to enemy bullets, something ingrained in him during the Civil War, finally caught up with him.

General Lawton was reviewing the disposition of his troops near San Mateo early in the morning of December 19th when a lone Philippine sniper opened up on General Lawton and his staff. A couple of bullets smacked into the ground nearby. Lawton's aides urged him to take cover. He scoffed at them stating, "I must see the battlefield." Moments later, the sniper took more careful aim. The full frame of General Lawton, all six foot five inches of him, plus his cream colored uniform and enormous pith helmet were perfectly framed in the morning light. A single round slammed into Lawton's chest.

Lawton clutched his heart, shouted, "I am shot!" and fell backward, dead. Almost unbelievably, the rebel Philippine officer who commanded the troops that killed General Lawton was a General named Geronimo.

Citation:

"Led a charge of skirmishers against the enemy's rifle pits and stubbornly and successfully resisted 2 determined attacks of the enemy to retake the works."

Chapter 7: Colonel Charles E. Phelps, 7th Maryland Infantry, US Army

Harvard Affiliation: Law School, JD- 1853

Col. Phelps, 1864

Charles Edward Phelps was born in Guilford, Vermont, May 1st, 1833. His father, John, was a lawyer and Vermont State Senator. The family moved to Pennsylvania in 1837 and subsequently to Maryland in 1841. His father set up a law practice in Baltimore and his mother, Almira, was selected to be principal of a local girl's academy.

When it came time to focus on Charles' education, his family selected Princeton, where Charles graduated in 1852. He immediately matriculated at Harvard Law School, from which he also graduated, in 1853.[8] Returning home to Maryland to practice law, he joined the Maryland Bar in 1855, was admitted to practice before the United States Supreme Court in 1859; and, in 1860, elected to the Baltimore City Council at age twenty-seven. He was a young man on the rise.

With hostilities looming in 1861, Phelps joined the Maryland Guard and was given the rank of Major. The Maryland Guard was established as a ceremonial unit, as were many of the local guard and militia units during the antebellum period. Many times these companies were nothing more than social clubs where men could fraternize and parade and preen in their military finery. The Maryland Guard, by all accounts, took their drills and maneuvers a bit more seriously: They were a fairly dedicated bunch.

When the war finally broke out, the Guard, just like the State of Maryland itself, was sundered by opposing loyalties. Most of the Guard's members "went South." Major Phelps stayed with the North and when the 7th Maryland Union Volunteer Regiment was raised in August 1862, Phelps joined it and became its Lieutenant Colonel.

The Regiment spent the balance of 1862 defending Maryland but then moved on and had a challenging 1863: There were extended operations against the enemy in West Virginia and the 7th fought in the Peach Orchard at Gettysburg. The 7th pursued Lee's army south, participated in

---

[8] Before the major, modern revisions of the 1870s, the Law School had rather less formal programs and--literally--no admissions requirements. Most lawyers of that era were still "reading for the law" in local offices rather than attending a formal law school.

the Bristoe Campaign, and fought at the battles of Bristoe Station, Haymarket, and Mine Run. When the 7th's Colonel was wounded, Phelps was promoted to Colonel and assumed command of the regiment.

As the 1864 campaign kicked off, the 7th was attached to General Gouverneur Warren's 5th Corps. In May, Grant began pressing in Lee's backyard and the first results were the battles in the Wilderness, where the 7th participated gallantly, but with great losses.

Colonel Phelps met his greatest challenge of the war on May 8th, 1864, at the Battle of Spotsylvania. This rolling juggernaut of a conflict lasted almost two weeks and racked up 32,000 casualties on both sides. There were moments of high drama and much bloody, brutal hand-to-hand combat. It all resulted in a tactical draw, except that Lee's army could ill-afford the losses that were inflicted upon it.

At the beginning of the battle, Confederate General Richard H. Anderson was in a blocking position vis-à-vis the two Union Corps of Generals Warren and John Sedgwick. Anderson was dug in at a place called Laurel Hill, near Spotsylvania Court House. Warren, mistakenly believing that he was facing only Confederate cavalry, ordered an all-out assault. It was a disaster.

By noon, the Union advance was bogged down near the crest of the hill. Confusion ranged all up and down the line. Units slugged it out, one against another, in ragged brawls of intense savagery. The 2nd Division, of which the 7th Maryland was a part, was hotly engaged. The Division commander was blown off his horse and lost a leg. His successor was blasted from his mount and lost an arm. The next senior officer was the Colonel of the 7th Maryland,

Charles Phelps. This is what happened next, in Charles Phelps's own words, written in the third person, as he penned them into the history of the 7th Maryland:

"Upon the fall of these two ranking officers, the command of the division, or what there was of it in sight (the two left brigades having been repulsed or mingled with the Maryland brigade), was promptly assumed by the Colonel of the Seventh Maryland. The situation, at that moment, was very plainly that of a forlorn hope, calling for nothing but quick and reckless work. What remained of the movement was no longer a column, but a bunched and ragged line. At points where the enemy's fire was most concentrated, the drone of bullets blended into a throbbing wail, like that of a sonorous telegraph wire pulsing in a strong wind, punctuated by the pert zip of the closer shots. The din and racket were such that but few could have heard the commands: "Hold your fire! Double quick!" What was plainly seen in front, was the sudden appearance of the new commander, pointing with saber to the breastworks, and trotting up towards them, until horse and rider came down."

Phelps was the "Colonel of the Seventh" to whom he refers and he was the officer "pointing the saber" and "trotting" toward the enemy until "horse and rider came down." What actually occurred, as witnessed by many and reported later, was that Phelps leapt upon his conspicuously white horse, and drew his sword. He started waving the sword over his head while yelling like a madman at the nearby men to rally to him. He gathered soldiers, hundreds of them, and led them forward in a desperate charge to within ten feet of the enemy's earthworks. Phelps was wounded in the chest and his horse was shot out from under him. Both went down in a heap.

51

It was an act of extreme rashness but incredible bravery, resulting in Phelps being awarded the Medal of Honor.

The men took the works, but seeing Phelps wounded and trapped beneath his dead horse, they wavered and fell back. The commander of "I" Company, a Captain Anderson, rushed forward to rescue his Colonel. As he tried to lever the horse off of Phelps, Anderson was struck three times by Rebel balls and went down, seriously wounded. Anderson's courageous and selfless act would net the young Captain a promotion to Lieutenant Colonel.

The Confederates re-took the summit and made Phelps and Anderson prisoners. The two men were taken to the rear of the Confederate lines. In the confusion of the continuing battle, the wounded duo were left alone and tried, twice, to escape, by re-crossing the lines. During the first attempt Phelps was shot again, but only slightly wounded in the left arm. During the second attempt, they were accosted by Confederate stragglers who robbed Phelps of everything of value he had upon his person.

Soon thereafter the battle subsided, temporarily, and the wounded men were escorted to a Confederate hospital. They received, according to Phelps, "proper (and) exceptional treatment" and were allowed to rest overnight.

The Confederate hospital was overrun by Union troopers from General Phil Sheridan's cavalry the very next day and Phelps and Anderson were repatriated. Amazingly, despite his wounds, Phelps was able to resume command of the 7th and lead his regiment at the Battle of Yellow Tavern on May 11th, three days later. It was at Yellow Tavern where General "Jeb" Stuart was finally out-fought and mortally wounded.

Phelps commanded his men again at Mechanicsville, on June 26[th,] but by September, he felt it was time to bow out and heal. He received a "surgeon's certificate of disability" and a brevet to Brigadier General.

The following November, Phelps was well enough to run for Congress. He was overwhelmingly elected, as an Unconditional Unionist, representing the 3rd Maryland District. He served two consecutive terms during which, in 1868, he married Martha Woodward of Baltimore. He was a brevet Brigadier General, war hero, and Member of Congress, all before he reached his 32nd birthday.

After his Congressional terms, he resumed his law practice in Baltimore, served a year as State Manager of the House of Reformation of Colored Children in Baltimore (1872); a stint as Commissioner of Public Schools; and, in 1892, he was appointed by the Governor of Maryland to the Baltimore Supreme Court—a position he held until 1908.

On March 30th, 1898, Phelps would finally receive the Medal of Honor he had earned in May of 1864. In 1907, Princeton would honor him with a doctorate. In 1908, the aging warrior went to his final rest and was buried in Baltimore's Woodlawn Cemetery.

Citation:

"Rode to the head of the assaulting column, then much broken by severe losses and faltering under the close fire of artillery, placed himself conspicuously in front of the troops, and gallantly rallied and led them to within a few feet of the enemy's works, where he was severely wounded and captured."

Chapter 8: Captain Horace Porter, Ordnance Department, US Army

Harvard Affiliation: Lawrence Scientific School, 1857

Brig. Gen. Porter, 1865

"Oh, the ignorance of us upon whom Providence did not sufficiently smile to permit us to be born in New England." so said the great American soldier, diplomat, and businessman Horace Porter. It is not known whether it was uttered tongue-in-cheek, but a serious researching of this man's life would seem to make it almost certain.

Horace Porter was born, instead in Huntingdon, Pennsylvania on April 15th, 1837. He had a privileged upbringing, part of which was spent in the Pennsylvania Governor's mansion when his father, David Rittenhouse Porter, served as the state's Chief Executive (1839-1845).

David Porter had been a very successful iron maker before entering politics. His son, Horace, gained a strong sense for manufacturing, engineering and science from his father; thus, when the young man's college education drew nigh, he selected the relatively new and somewhat controversial Lawrence Scientific School at Harvard University for his studies (1856-57).

Lawrence Scientific had been established in 1847 with a generous gift from the famous industrialist Abbott Lawrence. The school was an attempt to promote the engineering and physical sciences at Harvard, which had always been a noted bastion of the liberal arts. This radical departure from Harvard's historic curriculum had its ups and downs over the succeeding decades and would not become firmly established in the university's core programs until 1905 when Lawrence Scientific was transformed into the Graduate School of Engineering.

Nonetheless, in 1857, Lawrence Scientific was a bold, new engineering and sciences academy and Horace was drawn to its program. He stayed only a year, however, retiring in good standing. With hostilities looming, he requested and received a transfer to West Point, where he subsequently graduated 3rd in the Class of 1860.

At the Academy, he excelled in Ordnance and was detailed as an instructor at the Point immediately after his graduation. With the war clouds finally thundering in 1861, he was transferred to the Federal Army's critically important Watervliet Arsenal in Troy, New York.

After the war erupted, he was sent to Hilton Head, South Carolina, to scout out harbors for the Army and Navy. He was cited for gallantry in an action at Fort Pulaski, Georgia, in April 1862. This and his West Point training brought him to the attention of General McClellan who had him assigned to his staff. As a lowly first lieutenant he was, essentially, McClellan's Chief of Ordnance.

His prowess in the ordnance area and his skills at organizational structuring kept him busy. He was sent to the Department of the Ohio as Chief of Ordnance, then held the same post in the Army of the Cumberland, where he was promoted to captain. As a member of the General's Staff, it was typical for Porter to range over any battlefield his command fought on, and he was usually wherever the action was hottest.

Porter's warmest day in battle would be on September 20th, 1863, at the Battle of Chickamauga. This engagement was a disastrous defeat for the Union but it had its incredibly valorous moments, not the least of which was General Thomas' stubborn stand, an action that would earn him the nickname "the Rock of Chickamauga." While Thomas was trying to save the Army, a brave young captain was trying to rally a significant portion of it.

The center of the Union lines began to collapse on a high ridge above the battlefield. A reserve Corps of 5,000 men, under General Gordon Granger, was rushing forward to plug the hole that was developing but it was obvious they could not get there in time, unless the line were to somehow stop collapsing and hold until Granger could arrive.

Assistant Secretary of War Charles Dana was present on the battlefield that day. He had travelled from Washington at President Lincoln's request to make a report on the status of the forces under General Rosecrans. He happened to be near the center of the lines, woefully watching yet another rout of a major Union Army. As he gazed across the vista of the unfolding disaster, he saw something astonishing. Here is part of Dana's observation, as he wrote in his report to President Lincoln:

"Rosecrans went off, I don't know where; and the first sight that had any consolation in it was an officer with his sword drawn halting the fugitive soldiers of our army. He would halt them and form them into line and when he got twelve or twenty men together, a cannon-ball would come into their group right over our heads and they would fall. As soon as he would get another lot together, they would be swept down in the same manner."

The officer Dana observed was Captain Porter who somehow, in the middle of the action, and never being injured, rallied small groups of men, over and over, just enough to delay the oncoming Confederate onslaught.

Here is how Porter saw the action, in his own words:
"The roar of artillery and musketry and shouting of the men, the shrieking of a high wind through the trees made it a place to try the strongest of nerves...It took all our reserves to repulse the enemy and they did it handsomely...About eleven o'clock they came down on our centre . . . [Gen.] Gordon Granger was hurrying 5,000 men from the rear but they did

not reach us. Our centre came rolling back and the shells and bullets were sweeping everything from the earth . . .Getting to the crest of the hill, I met Drouillard (Captain James P. Drouillard), who had been with me at West Point. I told him I was going no farther, as long as we could hold ten men together."

Porter saved a large portion of the line from folding completely and his actions that day would later garner for him a belated Medal of Honor (1902).

Porter would be brevetted to Lieutenant Colonel for Chickamauga and a week after the battle would find himself on the staff of General Grant, where he would remain for the balance of the war. As Grant's military secretary, he would be present at Appomattox and witness the surrender of General Lee; and, in a final reward for his wartime services, Porter would receive another brevet, to Brigadier General, on March 13th, 1865.

After the war, Porter stayed in the Army and continued to serve as an aide-de-camp to Grant. Porter was an Assistant Secretary of War from August 1867 to January 1868, when Grant was the interim Secretary of War. After Grant was elected President in 1868, Porter held the post of Executive Secretary during Grant's first term (1869-1873).

In one of Porter's finest hours, he refused a half-million dollar bribe from Wall Street financier Jay Gould during Gould's 1869 attempt to corner the gold market. He reported the attempted bribe directly to Grant who, in turn, released enough Treasury gold holdings to un-do the attempted scheme.

By 1873, Porter had had enough of Army and political life. He resigned his commission and his post in Grant's White

House and went to work as a Vice President of the Pullman Railroad Car Company. He was associated with Pullman for twenty-four years, a period of time in which both he and the company prospered financially.

After his presidency, Grant went into the investment banking business in New York City but was financially ruined by a dishonest partner. Porter had maintained his friendship with Grant so he and others—notably Mark Twain—came to Grant's aid by assisting him with writing and promoting his memoirs. This three-volume bestseller, completed days before Grant's death in 1885, restored the Grant family fortunes.

After Grant's death, an elaborate monument was planned, but donations came in slowly. Porter stepped to the fore for his old friend once again and finished raising the money needed to build and dedicate Grant's Tomb in 1897.

Porter supported William McKinley for President in 1896 and was rewarded for his efforts with the Ambassadorship to France, a post he held for eight years, well into Theodore Roosevelt's Presidency. While Ambassador to France, Porter carried out what some thought was an odd and almost Quixotic search for the final resting place of America's first Naval hero, John Paul Jones.

After Jones' had served the fledgling United States, he went to Russia, where he was made an admiral in the Russian Navy. He did well for the Empress Catherine, but he could not stomach the palace intrigues, the jealousies of the native Russian princes and the inept but politically connected senior naval officers. He quit Russia in disgust in 1790 and returned to Paris. He did not find satisfactory employment until two years later when he received an appointment to become the

United States Consul to Algiers. Before he could get to his post, however, he died suddenly of kidney failure.

Jones was buried in a cemetery that belonged to the French Royal Family. After the French Revolution, the entire plot was turned into a vegetable garden, then later a place to dump dead animals and; finally, an arena where various animal fights were held.

Porter, using his own money, doggedly tracked the successive land ownership documents and bits of official correspondence until he discovered the designation of Jones' resting place and its probable location. Hiring an anthropologist, using sounding probes, and conducting exhaustive post-mortems of five possible coffins, Jones' remains were finally located and identified. The body was returned to the United States with full military honors and rests today in an ornate marble sarcophagus at the United States Naval Academy.

Horace Porter may have been born into a life of privilege, but he earned fame and fortune through his own incredibly dedicated efforts. He also lived a long and meaningful life, dying in New York on May 29th, 1921, at the age of 84.

Porter is not well remembered today, and that is unfortunate. He did much for his country. He also had a keen appreciation for history and what he envisioned for the nation's future. In 1907, he predicted that "the next war will be under the water and over our heads." He also said, in a memorable speech given at his alma mater, West Point, in 1902: "War should be undertaken only in the interest of peace. Upon our national arms, the American eagle is represented as holding in one talon the olive branch of peace and in the other the shafts of war. He leaves his adversaries which to choose."

Citation:

"While acting as a volunteer aide, at a critical moment when the lines were broken, rallied enough fugitives to hold the ground under heavy fire long enough to effect the escape of wagon trains and batteries."

Chapter 9: Captain Hazard Stevens, Assistant Adjutant General, 3rd Division, 9th Corps, US Army

Harvard Affiliation: AB, 1864 (1860); Honorary MA; 1906

Hazard Stevens, 1865

Popular literature, magazines and motion pictures have all enshrined George Armstrong Custer as the "Boy General of the Civil War;" and, indeed, he was vaulted from Captain straight to Brigadier General in 1865, at the age of 26. He was not, however, the Civil War's youngest General. That distinction belongs to Hazard Stevens who was brevetted a Brigadier on April 2nd, 1865, two months before his 23rd birthday.

Hazard was the son of Isaac Stevens, first Territorial Governor of Washington and himself a Major General of volunteers in the Civil War. Unfortunately, with his son fighting by his side, Isaac was cut down by a fatal ball to the head while rallying his brigade at the Battle of Chantilly, September 1st, 1862.

This ended a close-knit partnership of a father and a son that had already garnered enough adventure for many lifetimes. Hazard had been all over the Washington Territory with his father, roughing it, trying to obtain treaties with the various resident Indian tribes. It was tough and dangerous work and had once even erupted into an outright war, in which both father and son were combatants (1856-57). The following year, (1858) Isaac Stevens was elected to Congress and Hazard was sent off to the Chauncey Hall School in Boston, a preparatory academy for young men who particularly wished to matriculate at Harvard.

New England was not unfamiliar territory to Stevens. He had been born in Newport, Rhode Island on June 9th, 1842. The Hazard family roots in Rhode Island went back to the late 1600s.

After Chauncey Hall, Hazard went to Harvard, joining the Class of 1864, but he only spent one year in Cambridge. Like many young men of his day, he would drop out to join up as soon as the Civil War commenced.

His father resigned from Congress, was commissioned a Colonel, and was given command of the 79th New York Highlanders. Hazard went immediately to join his father and enlisted in the 79th. He did not shoulder a rifle for long, however. After a couple of skirmishes, wherein Hazard proved his worth, he was moved up to Adjutant for his regiment. A month later, has was made Captain and Assistant Adjutant of the brigade, then commanded by his recently promoted father, who had been made a Brigadier General.

The Stevens' fought together through most of 1862, including Second Bull Run and the fateful day at Chantilly, in September. Hazard was severely wounded in the left arm and left hip during the battle in which his father was killed. He was evacuated from the battlefield by a friend who commandeered an ambulance for the stricken Captain. Stevens was sent home to Newport for several weeks of rest and recovery.

Hazard rejoined the Army in time for the debacle at Fredericksburg (December 11-15, 1862). As part of General Gordon Getty's Corps he was named Inspector General of the 3rd Division, which had the dubious distinction of being the last futile wave thrown at the Confederates at Marye's Heights. Stevens was not injured in this battle but once again gave a good account of himself.

After the brutal winter of 1862-63, Steven's division was on the move, in March, to Suffolk, Virginia, to reinforce the Federal garrison stationed there. The Union men were facing the forces of General James "Old Pete" Longstreet. The next few weeks witnessed a series of see-saw moves between the opponents as they ranged up and down the James River, one side constantly trying to outmaneuver, outflank, or out-fortify the other.

The Confederates erected one particular redoubt they named Fort Huger. It was garrisoned by a couple of hundred troops but more troublesome were the five guns mounted in the fort. All attempts to destroy the Rebel cannons or knock out the fort by counter-battery fire or Navy gunboats had failed. Captain Stevens and a Navy Lieutenant by the name of

Roswell Lamson hatched a bold plan to storm the fort. They presented their scheme to General Getty who enthusiastically gave them the go-ahead.

The plan called for one gunboat to be packed with as many infantrymen as possible, about 270 men in all. The crew then erected a canvas screen all around the gunboat effectively keeping the troops out of sight. The gunboat, captained by Lamson, made a charge down the river as if it were about to try and run the gauntlet and get by Fort Huger. The Confederates double-shotted their guns in anticipation of blowing the gunboat out of the water as it sailed past. They held their fire to achieve maximum effect, which was just what Stevens and Lamson had hoped they would do.

As the gunboat approached the fort, it suddenly swerved to the bank near the base of the fort and stuck hard. The men boiled out of the boat, Captain Stevens in the lead, waving his sword and racing up the sides of the fort. The stunned Confederates had no time to react. The Union men hit the Rebels on the run and although they suffered four killed and ten wounded, they captured every Confederate in the fort and all the guns. General Getty had gone along for the ride and observed the entire affair. This bold attack would result in the award of the Medal of Honor for Stevens but not Lamson: The US Navy did not approve the Medal for officers until 1864. Even Stevens would not receive his Medal of Honor until much later (1894).

Stevens fought gallantly through the remainder of the war. He had horses shot out from under him and he was wounded yet again, by shrapnel, at the Battle of the Wilderness. He rose, successively, to Major (October 1863), Lieutenant

Colonel (August 1864), Colonel (October 1864); and, at Petersburg, Brigadier General (April 1865).

When he was ready to be mustered out of the Army in September 1865, he was offered a commission as a major in the Regular Army. He declined stating he had a widowed mother and three sisters to support and an Army major's pay was deemed insufficient. He ventured back to Washington where he obtained employment as an agent for the Oregon Steam Navigation Company. This led to an appointment as the government's Collector of Internal Revenue for the Territory. He built a house for his mother and sisters and started to read for the law. By 1870 he had been admitted to the bar and was appointed attorney for the Northern Pacific Railroad. In 1874, President Grant appointed Stevens the commissioner to investigate claims of British and United States citizens along the newly negotiated national border through the San Juan Straights.

Stevens was busy and successful, but he had more mountains to climb, figuratively and literally. In 1870 he took it upon himself to do something no one had yet done: climb to the top of Mt. Rainier. At 14,500 feet, Mt. Rainier is the highest peak in the lower forty-eight. Many had tried to get to the summit, but no one had succeeded. Local Indians said that the winds and snows were so strong at the pinnacle that anyone who got close would be swept into the air and lost forever. Stevens almost was, but on August 17th, 1870, he and a single climbing companion finally stood on the summit. It was late in the day, however, and the weather closed in on the men. They were saved from freezing to death that night by the fortuitous discovery of a small cave that was emitting steam from deep within the crater. It was quite a feat of mountaineering.

Due to the serious illness of one of the sisters, the Stevens family relocated to Boston in 1875 and Hazard followed them a year later. He took up the practice of law in Dorchester, where he built another home for himself and his family. He ran as an Independent for the Massachusetts State Legislature in 1885 and was elected, serving two terms.

Stevens lived the remainder of his life in Massachusetts but he returned annually to Washington. He had started a large and profitable dairy there, Cloverfields, and he stayed active in the business right up until his death. He even climbed Mt. Rainier one more time, in 1905, at the age of 63.

Stevens wrote a well-received book on the life of his father, continued to care for his family, never married, and ran for Congress in 1908 (he did not win). Harvard University, in recognition of his life of achievement, conferred an honorary Masters of Arts degree on him in 1906. The "boy general" turned into a venerable and respected "old warrior," and he died, after a full and eventful life, at age 77, in 1918.

Citation:

"The President of the United States of America, in the name of Congress, takes pleasure in presenting the Medal of Honor to Captain & Assistant Adjutant General Hazard Stevens, United States Army, for extraordinary heroism on 19 April 1863, while serving with U.S. Volunteers, in action at Fort Huger, Virginia. Captain Stevens gallantly led a party that assaulted and captured the fort."

Civil War Medal of Honor, circa 1863

Current Day Medal of Honor

The Battle of Five Forks, April 1, 1865
First Lt. Wilmon Blackmar earned his MOH during this fight

Gen. Phil Sheridan rallies the troops at Five Forks
Lt. Blackmar conducted a similar maneuver to earn his Medal

The Battle of Antietam, September 17, 1862
"The Bloodiest Day in American History"
and where Dr. Curran earned his MOH

A typical Union field hospital, similar to the one Dr. Curran
used as his surgery and recovery area

The Battle of Atlanta
Gen. Manning Force was gravely wounded
during this battle while earning his MOH

Judge Force, 1885
Evidence of his grim facial wound had faded by this time

The 150th Pennsylvania, in camp, April, 1862

The Gettysburg monument to the 150th Pennsylvania
including the McPherson stone barn: the site where Lt. Col.
Huidekoper made his brave stand

Capt. Henry Lawton, 1863
at 6-foot-five he was called "Long Hank"

The rifle pits in front of Atlanta where Capt. Lawton earned
his MOH with the 30th Indiana (photo circa 1910)

A charge like this at Spotsylvania earned Col. Phelps his
MOH

Judge Phelps-1895

The Union high point at Chickamauga where Gen. Thomas
made his stand, and Capt. Porter rallied the army, earning him
his MOH

Ambassador Porter, 1904
in the Theodore Roosevelt administration

a drawing of Ft. Huger, where Capt. Hazard Stevens earned
his MOH

Hazard Stevens (l) and Philemon von Trump (r) holding the
flag they took with them on their 1870 ascent to the top of Mt.
Rainier, the first to conquer that mountain

The Indian Wars
Chapter 10: Assistant Surgeon Leonard Wood, 4th Cavalry, US Army

Harvard Affiliation: Medical School; MD, 1884

Maj. Gen. Wood, 1917

A young doctor, two years out of Harvard Medical School, accompanied Captain Henry Lawton (see Chapter 6) and his ragged band of cavalrymen as they completed a 3,000 mile back-and-forth trek across the American Southwest in search of the renegade Apache, Geronimo in 1886. He shared all their privations including blistering sun, freezing nights, constant hunger, hit-and-run fights, chronic fatigue, and several bouts of intestinal ailments. In addition, he was bitten by a tarantula. The bite caused intense pain, fevers, aches, severe swelling and required the doctor to operate on himself, not once but several times, to save his own life. Through a gritty determination that even the tough-as-nails Lawton noted was exceptional, the assistant surgeon survived and soldiered on.

Once recovered, he embarked on a solo, harrowing, night-and-day, 100-mile, non-stop slog through hostile territory to deliver critical dispatches. He also, at one point in the expedition, due to a shortage of line officers, voluntarily took command of a detachment of infantry, a highly unusual turn of events for a doctor.

Then again, Leonard Wood was a highly unusual individual: driven, ambitious, intensely loyal, brilliant, and politically savvy, he turned his Indian Territory adventures into a Medal of Honor. Soon after earning his Medal, Wood was promoted to Captain and assigned to the White House as the personal physician to the President. Along the way he also met another talented and motivated young man, Theodore Roosevelt, and the two became fast friends. It was an association that would carry both of them onward and upward to the pinnacles of power.

Wood was born in Winchester, New Hampshire, on October 9th, 1860, the son of a successful physician who served with great distinction during the Civil War. He was raised to respect and emulate traditional New England values which included frugality, simplicity, moral rectitude and intense patriotism; qualities he adhered to throughout his life. He had a hard side, too, and it was one that drove him, some said relentlessly, and caused him to be perceived as egotistical, stubborn and intensely manipulative. There was no doubt he was a complicated man, and one who had flaws, but at the end of his life, his list of accomplishments was long and impressive.

His initial ambitions were for a military career, and he tried hard to gain admission to West Point or Annapolis, but failed to obtain an appointment to either school. Emulating his revered father, he decided the next best path was to obtain a medical degree, which he did, from Harvard, in 1884. Shortly after graduation, he saw an advertisement for the Army as a commissioned surgeon.

The young Captain was still the attending physician at the White House when the Spanish-American War broke out. Roosevelt finagled an appointment to a regiment of cavalry; but, feeling he didn't have the necessary experience, he talked the Department of the Army into giving his friend Wood the top spot, as a Colonel of Volunteers, and he took the post of second-in-command, as Lieutenant Colonel.

History will record their adventures in Cuba with the "Rough Riders" in glowing terms. After the war, Roosevelt was elevated to Governor of New York, Vice President and then President. Wood was propelled into the Governor Generalship of Cuba, a dramatically successful partnership with Walter Reed in conquering the dreaded yellow fever; and, when Roosevelt unexpectedly became President, he was promoted from Captain directly to Brigadier General in the Regular Army. It was an astonishing leap in grade that rankled many of the officers over whom he was "jumped."

After a controversial tour in the Philippines, where Wood was responsible for suppressing a native uprising— some say too brutally—he was recalled to Washington by his patron, President Roosevelt, and made the Chief of Staff of the

Army: he became the first and only medical officer to ever hold that post.

In his role as Chief of Staff, most historians agree that Wood was brilliantly innovative, extremely focused on the job, and intensely dedicated. He began what would become the Reserve Officers Training Corps, slashed many of the old bureaucratic structures that had kept the Army from modernizing and promoted many junior officers who were young, ambitious and talented. His actions, however beneficial, came at a price. Wood made many enemies among the members of "the establishment." He also made the fatal error—for a military careerist—of thinking he was immune from having to deal with the system that had allowed him to rise so high. He was a political general, never afraid to appeal directly to the public (and the media) or to his patrons if he needed a change that "the system" would not like. He also had a noted disdain for civilian authority. Some in Washington thought this made him a potentially dangerous man.

By the time the First World War touched America, Wood's old friend, Roosevelt, had been out of the White House for six years and Wood's numerous military and political enemies were holding the reins of government. Wood was desperate to command the American Expeditionary Force going to France—but he was pushed aside and passed over in favor of General "Black Jack" Pershing. Wood was given an important but decidedly non-glamorous training command.

While still in uniform, he actively sought the Republican nomination for the Presidency in 1920. He was outmaneuvered in his quest by the party regulars who ended up nominating a pliable patronage favorite, Senator Warren Harding. After Harding won the election, Wood made no secret of his ambition to made Secretary of War. All the new President would offer Wood was the post of Governor General of the Philippines. Wood accepted, although bitterly and reluctantly. Before taking up his new duties, he retired from the Army as a Major General, second only to Pershing in seniority.

The years in the Philippines (1921-1927) were marked by unhappiness, controversy and nagging headaches. The headaches turned out to be the recurrence of a brain tumor that Wood had initially beaten, via surgery, some ten years before. He needed surgery again but this time he died on the operating table on August 7, 1927. He is buried in the Rough Riders' section of Arlington National Cemetery.

Citation:

"Voluntarily carried dispatches through a region infested with hostile Indians, making a journey of 70 miles in one night and walking 30 miles the next day. Also for several weeks, while in close pursuit of Geronimo's band and constantly expecting an encounter, commanded a detachment of Infantry, which was then without an officer, and to the command of which he was assigned upon his own request."

The Spanish American War

Chapter 11: Lieutenant Colonel Theodore Roosevelt, First Volunteer Mounted Cavalry, US Army

Harvard Affiliation: AB, 1880

Col. Roosevelt, 1898

In the annals of great American men and women, there is hardly a more prominent, more accomplished name than Theodore Roosevelt. In his too-short 61 years of life, he did it all—and generally did it well.

His story is well-known, and it has been chronicled many times, most recently in the three-volume, Pulitzer Prize winning opus of Edmund Morris. For the sake of consistency with the other biographies contained herein, here is Roosevelt's abbreviated chronology:

He was born into a wealthy and prominent New York family in 1858. A sickly, asthmatic child, he spent most of his younger years trying to build up his strength and overcome his physical challenges. He succeeded brilliantly and remained hyperactive and athletic the remainder of his life.

As a young man, he was told he had a serious heart condition. He calculated he had roughly forty years to live, so he set out to cram as much adventure and accomplishment into his expected life span as was humanly possible. This may help explain why he was such a whirlwind—and such an exceptional success.

Because of his health, young "Teedie," as his family called him, was home-schooled. He was a good student, nonetheless, and able to matriculate at his first choice of college—Harvard—and went off to Cambridge in 1876. He graduated with the Class of 1880, 22nd out of 172 in rank. It was off to Columbia Law School, but he did not stay there long: he leapt at an unexpected chance to run for the New York State Assembly. He won the seat and his political career was launched. He never looked back. Twenty years later, he would be President of the United States, the youngest ever.

In between, Roosevelt was, at various times: a cowboy, soldier, naturalist, taxidermist, botanist, best-selling author, world-class hunter, avid conservationist, police commissioner, Governor of New York, Assistant Secretary of the Navy, and Vice President of the United States.

His flirtation with military greatness and the Medal of Honor began with that famous charge up San Juan Hill, Cuba, July 1st, 1898. A few months earlier, at the outbreak of the Spanish-American War, Roosevelt resigned as Assistant Secretary of the Navy to team up with his old friend, Leonard

Wood (see Chapter 10), to form the First U.S. Volunteer Cavalry Regiment. Wood became the regiment's Colonel with Lieutenant Colonel Roosevelt as second-in-command.

Roosevelt had never been in the military and knew nothing about the Army, but with his usual drive and tenacity, he learned quickly and his men idolized him. When one of the senior generals in the Cuban campaign became ill, Wood was promoted to Brigadier General and moved up. As a consequence, so did Roosevelt, who was promoted to Colonel and placed in command of the "Rough Riders," as their volunteer regiment was popularly called.

The "charge" up San Juan Hill, against Spanish soldiers who were entrenched at the top, wasn't a true cavalry dash: Roosevelt, at the time, was actually the only one on a horse. The main body of troopers, due to the terrain and barbed wire, were dismounted and running to the summit, firing as they went. This is not to diminish Roosevelt's bravery, which was extraordinary, but to put it in proper context. As the only soldier on horseback that afternoon, Roosevelt was a tremendously visible presence. He dashed from rifle pit to rifle pit urging the men forward, rallying each and every group, pushing the men ahead and moving them up the hill. He directed the assault most of the way and it was a true miracle that he was not shot out of the saddle.

Near the top, Roosevelt was finally forced to dismount: his horse was exhausted and the barbed wire was too dense. He led the troops the rest of the way on foot, and the Americans carried their objective. Later, Roosevelt was to call July 1st "the great day of my life;" and, "my crowded hour."

His courage was immediately recognized and Roosevelt was nominated for the Medal of Honor. Unfortunately, at that time, more of the Colonel's men were dying of malaria and the harsh Cuban conditions than were being killed in combat. Roosevelt wrote a scathing message on the poor treatment of the soldiers. The report was somehow "leaked" to the press which angered the Secretary of War and President McKinley. Shortly thereafter, Roosevelt's nomination for the Medal of Honor was disapproved. For the rest of his life, Roosevelt believed that his misdirected letter was the reason his award was declined, and he rued it bitterly.

He would, of course, go on to one of the most brilliant and successful presidencies in American history and also win the Nobel Peace Prize.

Once he left office and semi-retired to his estate at Sagamore Hill on Long Island, Roosevelt preferred to be called "the Colonel," never "Mr. President," and certainly not "Teddy," a nickname that he detested.

He tried to regain the presidency via the splinter Bull Moose Party in 1912, but failed. He also tried to convince President Wilson to make him a Brigadier General and let him lead a brigade to France during the First World War. Wilson politely but firmly declined: he did not need Roosevelt as a martyr, if were to be killed, or a potential rival (again), if he was to be successful.

The Colonel's poor health finally caught up with him and he died peacefully in his sleep, of a heart attack, on January 6th, 1919. It was said at the time, "Death had to take Roosevelt sleeping, for if he had been awake, there would have been a fight."

One fight did go on: getting Roosevelt the Medal of Honor. That battle was finally concluded successfully when Congressman Rick Lazio, representing Roosevelt's old home district on Long Island, re-introduced an updated recommendation to the Department of the Army in 1997. The award was finally approved in 2001 and Theodore Roosevelt was posthumously awarded his Medal of Honor. The Medal is on display in the Roosevelt Room at the White House.

Roosevelt is—so far—the only President to have received the Medal of Honor. He is also the only person who has ever been awarded this country's most prestigious award for valor in war and the world's greatest prize for peace.

Citation:

"For conspicuous gallantry and intrepidity at the risk of his life above and beyond the call of duty. Lt. Colonel Theodore Roosevelt distinguished himself by acts of bravery on 1 July, 1898, near Santiago de Cuba, Republic of Cuba, while leading a daring charge up San Juan Hill. Lieutenant Colonel Roosevelt, in total disregard for his personal safety, and accompanied by only four or five men, led a desperate and gallant charge up San Juan Hill, encouraging his troops to continue the assault through withering enemy fire over open countryside. Facing the enemy's heavy fire, he displayed extraordinary bravery throughout the charge, and was the first to reach the enemy trenches, where he quickly killed one of the enemy with his pistol, allowing his men to continue the assault. His leadership and valor turned the tide in the Battle for San Juan Hill. Lieutenant Colonel Roosevelt's extraordinary heroism and devotion to duty are in keeping with the highest traditions of military service and reflect great credit upon himself, his unit, and the United States Army."

<u>Vera Cruz, 1914</u>

Chapter 12: Captain Walter N. Hill, 2nd Advanced Base, US Marine Corps

Harvard Affiliation: AB, 1904

Colonel Hill, 1938

Walter Newell Hill was a rare individual in many ways; certainly for attaining the Medal of Honor but also for his intense dedication and singleness of purpose. He was born in Haverhill, Massachusetts, September 29th, 1881, and, like many young men from Massachusetts at the time, grew up with a focus on New England traditions, including attending a good prep school and trying to get into Harvard. He did both, graduating from the venerable Noble & Greenough School and matriculating with the Harvard Class of 1904.

Military service, among Harvard men, has always been looked upon as an acceptable prerequisite on the ladder of success, especially during times of war or crisis, but rarely has it been chosen as a career path. Walter Hill graduated from Harvard in 1904, immediately accepted a commission as a Second Lieutenant in the Unites States Marine Corps and unerringly followed the Corps for thirty-four consecutive years. He attained steady promotion and served in various posts in Mexico, the West Indies, the Philippines, and was sent to France in WW I. He retired in 1938, as a Colonel, but was placed on the retired list as a Brigadier General in recognition of his having been awarded the Medal of Honor.[9]

In 1914, young Captain Hill found himself on a troop transport headed to Vera Cruz, Mexico, commanding a company of Marines. The battle of Vera Cruz, which took place over two days in April, 1914, was a result of a diplomatic dust-up that served only one primary purpose: to wield that "big stick" that recently retired President Roosevelt had spent so much time discussing during his two terms in office.

By this time, of course, the man holding the stick was President Woodrow Wilson. Vera Cruz happened mostly as a result of the United States intending to impose its will on the outcome of the 1914 Mexican Revolution. Affairs south of the border of the United States have always been of great concern,

---

[9] From 1925 until 1959 Navy, Marine Corps, and Coast Guard officers who had served with distinction, and had received a "valor award" (Silver Star or higher) were allowed to retire one rank higher than their terminal rank; thus Col. Hill having been decorated with the MOH, was advanced to Brigadier General upon retirement.

starting with the Mexican War of 1848. In 1914, diplomatic ties between the two countries had hit another low and to make matters worse, the government of Kaiser Wilhelm II of Germany was threatening to become involved, in opposition to the interests of America.

To intercept what was believed to be a large shipment of arms going to the rebels, President Wilson ordered the Navy and the Marines to occupy the port of Vera Cruz, seize the weapons, and try and stabilize the situation on behalf of the legitimate President of Mexico. On the morning of April 21st, 1914, over 500 Marines and nearly 300 Navy Bluejackets[10] stormed ashore. The landings were not seriously opposed, but soon large crowds of armed civilian rebels, groups of dissident soldiers and the cadets of the Mexican Naval Academy got into the fight.

Over the course of that day and the next, the Marines and sailors progressively took over the entire city. There was not one, decisive engagement but rather many small and determined struggles. Steadiness of purpose, excellent leadership, and tenacity would carry the day and that is exactly how Captain Hill earned his Medal.

For deeds of valor conducted over a period of only two days, the Secretary of the Navy elected to confer an astonishing 59 Medals of Honor. Many, at the time, thought this was a bit excessive for the 2,300 men engaged. Captain Hill's courageous actions were witnessed by many, however, and there was no disputing his eligibility.

---

[10] The US Navy, until the 1970s, maintained units of naval infantry called "Bluejackets." As opposed to the US Marines who were to defend the ship or storm ashore and fight, the Bluejackets were most often used for projecting naval gunfire and artillery ashore.

Hill was promoted to major in 1917, and was sent to France in early 1918. He made lieutenant colonel in 1926, and full colonel in 1934. As mentioned above, he retired in 1938 as a brigadier general.

He was recalled to active duty in 1942 and served until the end of WW II, at Marine Corps Headquarters, in Washington, DC. One goal, one career, one purpose, one life well-lived.

General Hill was married to the former Mary Fitzpatrick and the couple had a son and a daughter. Hill finally retired for good in 1945. He and Mary lived a quiet and comfortable life in New York City where this brave and dedicated officer died peacefully in his sleep on June 29, 1955, at age 74.

Citation:

"For distinguished conduct in battle, engagements of Vera Cruz, 21 and 22 April 1914. Capt. Hill was in both days' fighting at the head of his company, and was eminent and conspicuous in his conduct, leading his men with skill and courage."

1916

Chapter 13: Lieutenant Claud Jones, US Navy: Engineering Officer, USS Memphis, CA-10

Harvard Affiliation: MS, 1913

Adm. Jones, 1945

Claud Jones was born October 7th, 1885, and came out of the hills of West Virginia in 1903 to enter the Naval Academy. He graduated with the Class of 1907 and during the time he attended Annapolis he studied alongside a number of men who would become household names during WW II: "Bull" Halsey

('04), Chester Nimitz ('05), Frank Fletcher and Raymond Spruance (both Class of '06).

Unlike the "Fighting Admirals" of WW II, Claud Jones' date with destiny and the Medal of Honor would come before either WW I or WW II. It was, in fact, during a tsunami, off the coast of Santo Domingo in 1916.

In the early 1900s the young men who graduated from the Naval Academy weren't automatically commissioned. Instead, they spent their first one or two years as graduated Midshipmen. So it was for Jones who, in 1907, went out to the fleet and served in the battleships *Indiana* and *New Jersey* before receiving his commission as an Ensign in 1908. Setting his compass in a specific direction, he went back to the Naval Academy in 1911 for advanced training in electrical engineering and while there, he also cross-trained at Harvard, where he earned a Master of Science degree in 1913.

Newly promoted to Lieutenant, Jones reported aboard the *USS Memphis*, an armored cruiser, in 1915 as the Engineering Officer. On August 29th, 1916, the *Memphis* was rocking gently, at anchor, in the roadstead off Santo Domingo, the Dominican Republic, when about 3:00 p.m. the skies suddenly darkened and the ocean began to behave strangely.

Unbeknownst to the crew, in those days before early warning devices, an underwater earthquake somewhere in the Atlantic had generated a giant tidal wave, or tsunami. The wave was hurtling straight toward Santo Domingo. The *Memphis'* Captain was ashore. The Executive Officer became alarmed at the state of the oceanic conditions he was seeing. The ship was on minimal steam. He ordered Lieutenant Jones, to get steam up as rapidly as possible so the ship could slip its anchor and get out to sea.

Even with super-human effort, it would take more than half an hour to get the boilers fired up and able to put out enough pressure to power the ship to safety. Unfortunately, the wave arrived first.

Titanic breakers began to pound the warship, rolling it heavily. Water poured through every opening, even spilling into the ventilators and the ship's four tall smokestacks. Below decks, the engineers were tossed about wildly. The boilers broke free from their fittings and spewed deadly, scalding vapors over the engine room and the men entrapped within. Lieutenant Jones was seriously injured but began pushing, shoving and dragging his men from the doomed spaces to get them to safety.

The ocean, which would normally have been twenty-five feet below the ship's keel, was suddenly sucked away. The *Memphis* struck bottom and the main tidal wave slammed into her. She was carried directly onto the rocky coast about a half mile away, smashed onto the rocks and stranded.

More than forty men were lost, including several who had inhaled deadly steam or had been burned so badly they could not survive. It was clear, however, that the losses, especially among the engineers, would have been much worse had it not been for the bravery of Lieutenant Jones. It would take another sixteen years, but Jones would finally receive his Medal of Honor from President Hoover in a White House ceremony in 1932.

After the loss of the *Memphis*, Jones was posted to the Brooklyn Navy Yard to work with the Westinghouse Machine Company on the building of the battleship *USS Tennessee*. From 1921 to 1924, Jones served at the Bureau of Engineering in Washington; from 1924 to 1925 he was Assistant Naval

Attaché in London; then, back to the Bureau of Engineering until 1929.

In the 1930s and through WW II, Jones continued to serve in engineering billets. He was promoted to Lieutenant Commander in 1918 and designated a specialty engineering officer. He made Commander in 1921, Captain in 1933 and Rear Admiral in 1941.

While many of his peers from the Naval Academy were battling Germany and Japan at sea, Admiral Jones was building the ships that would allow them to complete their missions. He served most of WW II as the head of the shipbuilding division at the Bureau of Ships. He also, for a time, headed procurement and material, an extremely critical job in the war effort. For his skill in that post, he was awarded the Legion of Merit.

Admiral Jones retired at the end of the war. He returned to his native West Virginia but had only three years to enjoy his retirement, dying at home in 1948, at the age of 62.

Citation:

"For extraordinary heroism in the line of his profession as a senior engineer officer on board the U.S.S. Memphis, at a time when the vessel was suffering total destruction from a hurricane while anchored off Santo Domingo City, 29 August 1916. Lt. Jones did everything possible to get the engines and boilers ready, and if the elements that burst upon the vessel had delayed for a few minutes, the engines would have saved the vessel. With boilers and steam pipes bursting about him in clouds of scalding steam, with thousands of tons of water coming down upon him and in almost complete darkness, Lt. Jones nobly remained at

his post as long as the engines would turn over, exhibiting the most supreme unselfish heroism which inspired the officers and men who were with him. When the boilers exploded, Lt. Jones, accompanied by 2 of his shipmates, rushed into the firerooms and drove the men there out, dragging some, carrying others to the engine room, where there was air to be breathed instead of steam. Lt. Jones' action on this occasion was above and beyond the call of duty."

Asst. Surgeon Leonard Wood, 1886, Ft. Huachuca,
preparing to leave on the Geronimo Trek during which
he would earn a MOH

Capt. Lawton, Surgeon Wood, Geronimo and his warriors
prepare to board the train to take them into exile-1886

Col. Theodore Roosevelt (center) atop San Juan Hill, Cuba,
after the Rough Riders historic charge-July 1, 1898

President Roosevelt dedicates the General Henry Lawton
Memorial, Indianapolis, June 20, 1907

A squad of "Leathernecks," like the Marines led by Capt.
Walter Hill at Vera Cruz, 1914, where Hill earned a MOH

At Vera Cruz soldiers, Navy Bluejackets, and Marines faced
house-to-house opposition to secure the city

The cruiser USS Memphis wrecked and on the rocks, August,
1916, after being swamped by a tidal wave

Cdr. Claud Jones (2nd from right) receives his MOH for his
heroics aboard USS Memphis. Presenting the Medal was
President Herbert Hoover (center)

World War I
Chapter 14: Captain George G. McMurtry, Jr., 2nd Battalion, 308th Infantry, 77th Division, US Army

Harvard Affiliation: AB, 1899

Major McMurtry, 1918

If there is such a figure as a "stereotypical Harvard man," George McMurtry, Jr., just might fill the bill, albeit a caricature from an earlier era. His father, George, Sr., was an up-from-poverty Irish immigrant who fled to America during the infamous potato famine (like Dr. Curran's family, see

Chapter 3). He came to America, founded a steel mill, and made a fortune.

George Jr., was born during America's Centennial Year, 1876, in Pittsburgh, Pennsylvania: His father was busy making millions in the steel business and George Armstrong Custer was about to get massacred in the Badlands.

George's ambitious father was determined to have his son get the best education possible; so, George was headed to Harvard. He got there, only to drop out and join the Rough Riders, as an ordinary private, as soon as the Spanish-American War broke out and Lieutenant Colonel Roosevelt started seeking Ivy League volunteers for his new regiment. He soldiered well and bravely in Cuba. The war was over quickly, and he went back to Harvard to finish up his studies in time to graduate with his class.

The steel business did not interest him, but the excitement of Wall Street and New York City did; so, he joined a stock broking firm. He did well enough to make partner in the firm by 1900.

Although in his early forties, and exempt from having to serve, he volunteered readily when the United States declared war against Germany in 1917. He was rather old to be a First Lieutenant, his rank when he finished officer training, but he quickly made Captain and by the time his outfit, the 2nd battalion of the 308th Infantry, was slogging through the mud of northern France in late 1918, he was the unit's acting commander. He was no longer the carefree, stockbroker playboy. This was serious fighting and tremendously dangerous.

McMurtry and Major Charles Whittlesey (see Chapter 15) would become the central figures in what became the legend of the "Lost Battalion." The tale of the Lost Battalion is a story of stubborn perseverance, incredible bravery, and great sacrifice mixed with tragic error, unnecessary loss of life, and senseless blundering. It all started on October 2nd, 1918, deep in the Argonne Forest in northeastern France.

In late September, the French and the Americans opened up a large joint offensive in the Meuse-Argonne region, the objective of which was to break the so-called Hindenburg Line. This battle would rage until the very end of the war (November 11th) and would be the bloodiest fight in the history of American arms. The Lost Battalion's momentous place in the history of this struggle occurred between October 2nd and October 7th.

On October 2nd, three battalions of the 308th Infantry Regiment along with the rest of the 77th Infantry Division were pushing through the Argonne Forest. Captain McMurtry commanded the 2nd Battalion of the 308th and Major Charles Whittlesey commanded the 1st Battalion of the same regiment. The vast majority of the corps-sized attack bogged down far from reaching their goals, but not Whittlesey's men. They reached their objective, Charlevaux Mill, and were soon joined by McMurtry's soldiers, plus K Company of the 3rd Battalion, commanded by Captain Nelson Holderman. Also breaking through to join this ad-hoc force were two companies of the 306th machine gun regiment, about 554 men in total.

As the offensive stalled, the division commander, Major General Robert Alexander, directed a retrenchment and nearly all the units returned to their original lines. McMurtry, Whittlesey, and Holderman never received the order to retreat. As a result, the salient that they had created soon became an isolated pocket completely surrounded by the Germans. To make matters worse, the Americans had started off with only one day's rations and no foul weather or overnight equipment.

The Germans were quick to see their advantage and leapt to the attack, trying to wipe out the isolated soldiers. The Americans dug in and fought back valiantly. Much of the fighting became hand-to-hand in the thickly wooded forest. The only means of communication between the trapped GIs and their Division was by carrier pigeon, and there were only a few birds on hand, at that.

The struggle went on for three days before Whittlesey was able to communicate his position to the rear and request artillery support. Unfortunately, and possibly due to a mistaken calculation made by Whittlesey (never confirmed), the coordinates were inexact and the devastating artillery barrage that followed fell mostly on the Americans. It took another four hours, and the last carrier pigeon, to get the artillery to cease fire. It was a deadly and very costly mistake.

The Americans had little water and less food and at several points resorted to pilfering rations from the German dead. Medical supplies were almost non-existent and the scarce bandages were also stripped from the dead to be re-used on the living wounded. Several planes were flown over what was believed to be the position of the Americans but the heavy forestation prevented direct observation. Almost all the food and ammunition dropped ended up in enemy hands.

On October 6th, the Lost Battalion got a break, albeit an ultimately tragic one. First Lieutenant Harold Goettler, a pilot with the Army Air Corps, and his observer, Second Lieutenant Erwin Bleckley, flying a DeHaviland DH-4, were finally able to get accurate observations and pinpoint the locations of both the Lost Battalion and the Germans. They turned to race for the American lines with their information but were taken under intense enemy fire. Goettler was shot in the head but the plane, somehow, crash-landed behind the Allied lines. Goettler was dead in the cockpit and Bleckley, who was thrown from the aircraft, died on the way to the hospital. The maps and notes Bleckley had made were recovered, however, and provided an accurate position for the Lost Battalion. Based on that information, a relief force was set in motion and the artillery opened up again, this time with a more favorable result.

The relief column arrived on the 7th. One-hundred ninety-seven of the original 554 had been killed. Another 150 or so were taken prisoner or were missing. Of the remaining 207, most were wounded and very few were capable of walking out of the forest under their own power—including Captain McMurtry. A German hand grenade had gone off near him and shattered a kneecap on October 4th and he had been struck again by shrapnel, in the shoulder, on October 6th.

It was a singular event of great courage in a savage and brutal war. Whittlesey, McMurtry, and Holderman survived and were decorated with the Medal of Honor, as were the two brave pilots who sacrificed their lives to find them. In further recognition of his valor, McMurtry was promoted to Major and received the Legion d'Honneur and the Croix de Guerre from the government of France.

After the war, McMurtry was back on Wall Street where he made an even bigger pile of money. Despite the Crash of 1929, he managed to keep his fortune and he finally retired in 1938. That year and every year thereafter, until his death, McMurtry hosted an annual Lost Battalion Reunion. Veterans came from all over the country—and McMurtry paid the entire bill, travel expenses and all, for everyone who attended. He enjoyed life to its fullest, bought a mansion in Bar Harbor, Maine, and told war stories with his old comrades until he died, in 1958, at the ripe old age of 82: He had quite a life.

Citation:

"Commanded a battalion which was cut off and surrounded by the enemy and although wounded in the knee by shrapnel on 4 October and suffering great pain, he continued throughout the entire period to encourage his officers and men with a resistless optimism that contributed largely toward preventing panic and disorder among the troops, who were without food, cut off from communication with our lines. On 4 October during a heavy barrage, he personally directed and supervised the moving of the wounded to shelter before himself seeking shelter. On 6 October he was again wounded in the shoulder by a German grenade, but continued personally to organize and direct the defense against the German attack on the position until the attack was defeated. He continued to direct and command his troops, refusing relief, and personally led his men out of the position after assistance arrived before permitting himself to be taken to the hospital on 8 October. During this period the successful defense of the position was due largely to his efforts."

Chapter 15: Major Charles W. Whittlesey, 1st Battalion, 308th Infantry, 77th Division, US Army

Harvard Affiliation: Law School, JD, 1908

Lt. Col. Whittlesey, France, 1918

Charles Whittlesey and George McMurtry (Chapter 14) were tested in the very same combat crucible and both received the Medal of Honor for the very same action, but their lives after that momentous event went in vastly different directions. Perhaps that was inevitable, for they were polar opposites from the very beginning.

Whittlesey was born in Florence, Wisconsin, in 1884, but as a young boy, his family moved to Pittsfield, Massachusetts, where his father had taken a mid-level job at the General Electric Company. A quiet, intelligent, and literary lad, he attended Williams College, close to home, and edited the college newspaper and yearbook.

After graduation from Williams in 1905, he went off to Harvard Law School and received his law degree from Harvard in 1908. In one of the few ways that his life would connect with McMurtry, other than the war, he, too, elected to seek his fortune in New York City, where he and a friend set up a law practice in 1911.

With the war coming on, Whittlesey decided he needed to do his part, so he volunteered for reserve officer training, which he completed in August 1916. He was activated a year later, in August, 1917, and sent to Camp Upton in Yaphank, Long Island. Camp Upton, at the time, was a major staging area for troops who would be going off to France.

Promoted to Captain, he was placed in charge of the Headquarters Company of the 308th Battalion of the 77th Infantry Division. After the 77th arrived in France, they soldiered behind the British for a time and then, when they were deemed ready to strike out on their own, in August 1918, Whittlesey was given command of the 1st Battalion of the 308th and elevated to Major.

As related in the chapter concerning Captain McMurtry, fate threw Whittlesey and his command far out in front of a doomed advance into the Argonne Forest in October, 1918. Some accounts praise Whittlesey for his drive and initiative in getting his troops to their objective. Others say Whittlesey's inexperience and inattention to the state of affairs with the rest of his Division caused his men to be too far in advance of their support and, thus, responsible for their own entrapment. Either way, there they were: stuck in a pocket of resistance, totally surrounded by the Germans.

The next six days were utterly desperate and intensely heroic and Whittlesey's leadership had much to do with a positive outcome. He could have surrendered with honor, and was asked by the Germans several times to do so. He stubbornly refused. At one point, though he later denied it, some of his men clearly heard Whittlesey tell the German courier who brought one surrender offer to "Go to hell!"

On October 4th, he risked calling down the American artillery on the Germans knowing full well, because of the closeness of the two lines, that there was a chance his own men could get caught up in the blasts. Unfortunately, they were, and as a result a number of Whittlesey's men were killed and wounded. It took an agonizing four hours to get the artillery to stop firing.

Whittlesey forever after blamed himself for that tragic mistake although there is only scant evidence that he was at fault—it could easily have been a mistake on the part of the artillery. No one has ever been able to say for certain.

History does record that until the Lost Battalion was finally relieved, on October 7th, Whittlesey, as the senior officer present, led his men in a gallant and heroic defense of their position under incredibly debilitating conditions. For his bravery, he, like Captain McMurtry, was awarded the Medal of Honor.

Whittlesey was advanced to Lieutenant Colonel and also awarded the Croix de Guerre. He left France in November, 1918, and returned to New York City where he was mustered out. He tried to pick up the threads of his law practice but found that he was too much in demand for speeches and appearances. He even participated in a 1919 movie about the "Lost Battalion" that included a number of his former comrades.

In 1921, he was promoted to Colonel and placed in command of the 308th Infantry Reserve Regiment. It was also during that year that the Tomb of the Unknown Soldier was dedicated in Washington, DC. Colonel Whittlesey was asked to be a pall bearer at the ceremony.

A few days after the ceremony, Whittlesey, without telling any of his family or friends, unexpectedly booked passage on a United Fruit Company steamship headed to Cuba. On the first night out, after dining amiably with the captain and the passengers, Whittlesey said he was retiring to his cabin.

Sometime during the night, far out in the Atlantic Ocean, Whittlesey jumped off the ship. His body was never found. He left no suicide note but did leave, in his cabin, detailed instructions for the captain on how to handle his luggage. He had also left letters behind containing instructions on what to do with his estate and how to execute his will. He bequeathed nearly everything to his mother but he did bequeath McMurtry the note from the German commander asking for their surrender, during one of the darkest days in the Argonne Forest.

Today, we might diagnose Colonel Whittlesey with what has become known as PTSD: Post Traumatic Stress Disorder. He was deeply affected by the events surrounding the Lost Battalion. He constantly agonized over the disastrous artillery attack on his men. He came to regret not surrendering, believing, after the fact, that if he had done so he would have saved many lives. He was distressed over the attention paid to him and the hero worship he felt he did not deserve. Just before his fatal trip he had remarked to his best friend, "Not a day goes by but I hear from some of my old outfit, usually about some sorrow or misfortune. I cannot bear it much more."

Citation:

"Although cut off for 5 days from the remainder of his division, Maj. Whittlesey maintained his position, which he had reached under orders received for an advance, and held his command, consisting originally of 46 officers and men of the 308th Infantry and of Company K of the 307th Infantry, together in the face of superior numbers of the enemy during the 5 days. Maj. Whittlesey and his command were thus cut off, and no rations or other supplies reached him, in spite of determined efforts which were made by his division. On the 4th day Maj. Whittlesey received from the enemy a written proposition to surrender, which he treated with contempt, although he was at the time out of rations and had suffered a loss of about 50 percent in killed and wounded of his command and was surrounded by the enemy."

World War II

Chapter 16: Major Pierpont Morgan Hamilton, US Army Air Corps

Harvard Affiliation: BA, 1920; AM, 1946

Major General Hamilton, 1958

When you are the great-great grandson of Alexander Hamilton and the grandson of J.P. Morgan, it would not be unreasonable for the world to expect great things of you. Perhaps your heritage might send you in the direction of becoming a great patriot, a distinguished military officer, or possibly even a banker of some renown. Pierpont Hamilton, Harvard Class of 1920, managed to become all three.

Tuxedo Park, New York, August 3, 1898: Pierpont Hamilton was born into one of the wealthiest families in America. His formative years, as one might imagine, lacked for very little in terms of material needs; yet, as those who knew him in later life would remark, the money and prestige seemed to have had little effect on his remarkably strong personality and his genuine ambition.

Typical of many young men from his social class in the early years of the 20th Century, he was packed off to boarding school as soon as he was eligible. In Pierpont's case the school was Groton and matriculation at Harvard followed in 1916.

With America's entry into the Great War in 1917, many Harvard undergraduates couldn't wait to get into the fight. Pierpont was one of them. He dropped out of Harvard and went off to Cornell, but only because the Ithaca campus was, at the time, the site of the Army's Aviation Ordnance School. Flight training at Hazelhurst Field in Hempstead, New York (now known as Roosevelt Field) and advanced flight training at Ellington Field in Texas followed. After graduating from Ellington, Hamilton was awarded his pilot's wings and commissioned a Second Lieutenant in the Army Reserve on May 18, 1918.

Hamilton's immediate goal was to get to France and get into the air war. The Army had different plans for him, however, as the Army often does. Instead of being sent overseas, he was kept at Ellington Field training newer pilots. There was a rumor that his influential family had played a role in keeping him out of combat. Six months later, with the war over, Hamilton was released from active duty. He returned to Harvard to complete his education and graduated with the Class of 1920. He married, for the first of three times, in 1919.

During the years between the World Wars, Hamilton settled comfortably into the family's investment banking business, first in Paris, then in New York. He learned to speak French fluently, an attribute that would have profound consequences on his later military adventures.

After Pearl Harbor Hamilton, although at age 43 exempt from military service, volunteered again. He was returned to active duty in March 1942, with the rank of Major. He was initially assigned to the Intelligence Section in Washington, DC, but in June of 1942, Hamilton was transferred to London to join the staff of Lord Louis Mountbatten. His main duty was to act as the American forces liaison to Mountbatten and to assist in planning commando raids into continental Europe.

One of Hamilton's first assignments was to work on what became known as the Dieppe Raid. Dieppe was a small French port on the English Channel and in August of 1942 it became the target of the Allies' first attempt to get back into enemy-held Europe. It was a disaster from beginning to end. The Allies learned a number of valuable lessons, but at a great cost in lives—mostly Canadian. The biggest lesson learned was that the Allies were not ready to conduct a major invasion of Europe; so, instead, it was decided to work up to the re-taking of the Continent by attempting a lesser but still strategically important target: North Africa.

Despite the poor outcome at Dieppe, Hamilton had proven himself to be an outstanding intelligence officer. He was recalled to Washington to immediately begin the intelligence work-ups for Operation Torch, the North African invasion, scheduled for October of that year.

The North African landings, in addition to being a much-needed rehearsal for the greater invasion of Europe, were going to be particularly thorny from an operations standpoint. The general plan called for the invasion of territory critical to the survival of Germany's plans for Africa; but, the majority of the defensive forces were French. France, of course, had fallen to Germany early in 1940 and had been controlled since then by the pro-German Vichy Government. No one knew, when the Allied armies arrived at the beaches of Morocco, if the French forces guarding the area would greet the invading forces as liberators or foes. The Americans planned to fight but hoped it wouldn't be necessary.

A critical part of the strategy called for landing a probing force at Port Lyautey, the gateway to Casablanca. The tactical units in the advance would attempt to rush forward, contact the French commanders, negotiate a truce, and lead a bloodless "liberation" of the entire area. Major Hamilton was selected for a lead role in this gamble along with Colonel Demas T. "Nick" Craw of the Army Air Corps. Both men spoke French. The first task for the two officers was to get on the beach, find the local French commander, a Colonel Charles Petit, and secure American access to the French airfield.

The operation to seize Port Lyautey and Casablanca, became known as "Operation Goalpost." The 1st, 2nd and 3rd Battalions of the 60th Regimental Combat Team from the 9th Infantry Division—about 9,000 men altogether—with a gaggle of light tanks and combat vehicles were designated as the assaulting force. They arrived off the coast on November 7th, just before midnight.

From this moment forward, the entire operation became a gigantic exercise in frustration, ineptness, and bad execution. First, the naval contingent, led by the *USS Texas*, confused the rest of the landing fleet by making a baffling course correction which sent the troop ships and their supporting warships all over the chart.

Second, the essential elements of the landing force and its coordinators had been split up among three different transport ships. The overall force commander, General Lucien Truscott, had to get ferried from ship to ship to coordinate troop movements. While all this was going on, a French steamer sailed by the invasion fleet and was able to signal the French defending forces that a landing was imminent.

Valuable time was lost in all the confusion and as a result, the Port Lyautey debarkations were delayed for over an hour. The last act in this comedy of military errors occurred when President Roosevelt and General Eisenhower's pre-recorded radio messages announcing the North African invasion went on the air as scheduled. General Truscott's men hadn't even boarded the landing craft that would ferry them to shore.

By the time the first Allied waves hit the beach, it was nearly 0600. The French decided to resist. Coastal batteries commenced a heavy fire on the landing craft forcing many to turn away from their intended disembarkation points. The US Navy opened up on the French batteries. Two French fighters flew over the beaches strafing the landing force. Into this maelstrom of artillery, rockets and bullets, Colonel Craw and Major Hamilton went ashore, undeterred. They carried with them copies of the President's radio broadcast and assurances that if the French allowed the Americans ashore peaceably, that an honorable truce could be quickly structured.

Since the French had fired first, the US Navy decided it was going to go ahead with a full-blown attack. Craw and Hamilton were stranded on the beach and effectively blocked from trying to complete their mission. Craw managed to get in radio contact with General Truscott, who was reluctant to let Hamilton and Craw proceed. Craw managed to change Truscott's mind, however, and the two emissaries commandeered a jeep and a driver, one Private Orris Correy, and commenced an attempt to thread through the tangled Allied and French battle lines and find the French commander.

Using occasional lapses in the gunfire and some considerable driving skill, Private Correy picked his way through the French lines. With the flags of the United States, France and a white banner of truce flying from the jeep, the three men managed to get inside the guns of the Casbah fortress. The French officer commanding the battery gave them safe passage to try and locate the French Commander who was reportedly some miles further back. The trio sped off again. Just outside the port, very near their goal, a hidden machine gun crew fired on the jeep from a concealed spot near the road. It was a purely defensive reaction to an "enemy" vehicle approaching their position. Unfortunately, the bullets struck Colonel Craw and ripped through his body. He was killed instantly. Correy and Hamilton were not hit, but Correy lost control of the jeep and slammed into a tree.

The French soldiers surrounded the jeep. Hamilton, in fiery French, angrily started to berate the men for firing on a flag of truce and killing his companion. Hamilton and Correy were, nonetheless, made prisoners and handed over. They were taken to the local French commander. Ironically, it was the very same officer, Colonel Petit, they had been seeking. Petit expressed remorse over the death of Colonel Craw but also stated he could not cease operations without approval from his superiors. He was at least willing to make contact with his commanding general and pass on the proposals, which he did.

The Americans continued to make steady progress against the French and Hamilton kept trying to make diplomatic inroads with his captors. After two more days of fighting and cajoling, the French commander, General Mathenet, asked Hamilton to arrange a meeting with General Truscott so that a cease fire could be negotiated. Fighting came to an end the next day, November 11th. Hamilton had, at last, achieved the objective that he and his deceased partner had so earnestly desired.

It quickly became clear that the bravery of Craw and Hamilton, and Hamilton's persuasive powers, had prevented prolonged fighting and had made a real difference in lives saved—on both sides. For his gallantry and persistence in this harrowing operation, Hamilton was promoted to Lieutenant Colonel and decorated with the Medal of Honor by President Roosevelt at a ceremony in the White House on February 19th, 1943. Colonel Craw was likewise awarded the Medal of Honor, posthumously.

Hamilton was later promoted to Colonel, in October, 1943, and spent the balance of the war in senior staff positions, mostly in Washington, D.C., working for the Assistant Secretary of War for Air. At his own request, he was released from active duty in December, 1945. He returned to Harvard to complete a Masters Degree in 1946 but soon thereafter discovered that he had grown quite comfortable in uniform and began to lobby for a return to active duty. His request was granted in February, 1947, and Colonel Hamilton was assigned to the Plans and Operations Division of the War Department General Staff.

His abilities as an administrator and strategic thinker were widely praised. By the end of 1948, he was promoted to Brigadier General. He remained on active duty until March 31, 1952, when he was released once more. General Hamilton stayed in the Air Force Reserve until 1959 and was even promoted during that period one last time, to Major General.

Following his retirement from the Air Force, he went back into the banking business near his chosen home of Santa Barbara, California. The old warrior and scion of two great American families lived peacefully, happily and comfortably until passing away on March 4, 1982, at 83 years of age.

Citation:

"For conspicuous gallantry and intrepidity in action above and beyond the call of duty. On 8 November 1942, near Port Lyautey, French Morocco, Lt. Col. Hamilton volunteered to accompany Col. Demas Craw on a dangerous mission to the French commander, designed to bring about a cessation of hostilities. Driven away from the mouth of the Sebou River by heavy shelling from all sides, the landing boat was finally

beached at Mehdia Plage despite continuous machinegun fire from 3 low-flying hostile planes. Driven in a light truck toward French headquarters, this courageous mission encountered intermittent firing, and as it neared Port Lyautey a heavy burst of machinegun fire was delivered upon the truck from pointblank range, killing Col. Craw instantly. Although captured immediately, after this incident, Lt. Col. Hamilton completed the mission."

Chapter 17: Brigadier General Theodore Roosevelt Jr., Deputy Commander, 4th Infantry Division, US Army

Harvard Affiliation: AB, 1909

Brig. Gen. Theodore Roosevelt, Jr., France, 1944

Like father like son? When it came to Theodore Roosevelt, Sr., and his eldest son, Theodore Roosevelt, Jr., in some ways; yes, but in other ways, no.

Ted, Jr., was born in 1887 just as his soon-to-be-famous father was beginning his ascendancy to power and the Presidency. Ted., Jr., had an older half-sister, Alice, but as the future President's namesake, he was the bearer of his father's greatest expectations. This would never be an easy burden for Ted, Junior, to bear.

Ted did adore his father, and did wish to emulate the "old man," but his natural gifts were not equal to his father's and his foray into politics would not bear the same fruit.

Ted, Jr., liked to be called "Teddy," unlike his father who hated that name, and Ted, Jr., would be known by "Teddy" all his life. He was slated for Harvard as soon as he was born, and he did attend; but, unlike his dad, who breezed through his studies, Teddy struggled. He worked hard, though, and did graduate with his class, in 1909, just after his father finished his second term as President.

Teddy decided to take a crack at the business world immediately after graduation and had short stints in both the steel and textile industries. He then gravitated to investment banking, and in finance he found his niche. He was a quick study and by the time America was readying to enter WW I, he had made a sizeable fortune. Teddy was, in fact, wealthier than his father who had never been particularly good at managing his finances.

War had broken out in Europe in 1914, as we know, and martial feelings began to stir in America, but very little was being done to prepare the army or navy for actual participation. General Leonard Wood (see Chapter 10) did start the Reserve Officers Training Corps, an effort to train and prepare at least a cadre of a few thousand officers if America decided to "get into it."

This ROTC was, at first, more like "summer camp" for America's young gentlemen. In 1915, a large site was organized in Plattsburg, New York. With Regular Army drill sergeants and a few Regular officers, the elite young men of America's first families flocked to attend, and paid their own expenses to boot. These cadets were given the rudiments of military training and leadership in an atmosphere that reminded many of the new and popular Boy Scout movement. Teddy and two of his younger brothers, Quentin and Archie, were eager participants.

When America declared for the Allies, in April, 1917, Teddy was commissioned a major and sent to France. He fought in numerous campaigns with well known names such as Cantigny, the Marne, The Meuse-Argonne Offensive, and Soissons. He was gassed and wounded and the intense dampness of the trenches advanced his arthritis, a condition that would plague him for the rest of his days.

Teddy proved to be one of the very best American battalion commanders and by the summer of 1918 he had been promoted to lieutenant colonel and made commander of the 26th Regiment of the 1st Division. Sadly, at about the same time, his younger brother Quentin was killed in an aerial battle behind German lines.

Teddy's courage garnered for him a Distinguished Service Cross plus France's Legion of Honor and the Croix de Guerre. At the end of the war he was a full colonel, the highest rank attained by his father.

After the war, Teddy went back into the investment banking business in New York but he would not be in it for very long. It was time to scratch his political itch. He ran for and was elected to the New York State Assembly (just like his father) and when Harding was elected President, in 1921, Teddy was appointed Assistant Secretary of the Navy (just like his father). It seemed that mirror-image, father-and-son careers were emerging, but a snag nearly derailed Teddy permanently.

The biggest American political scandal of the early 20th Century was the infamous Teapot Dome Affair of 1922. The ineffective Harding, who was not personally corrupt, saw his administration get caught with its hands in the public till. Harding's greedy Interior Secretary, Albert B. Fall, arranged for his cronies to obtain incredibly lucrative government oil leases in the Teapot Dome, Wyoming, oilfields for very little money—plus what they put in Fall's pocket. Unfortunately, Teddy Roosevelt was the government official who signed off on the transfer of the Navy's portion of the leases. Although never accused of or prosecuted for any wrongdoing, it was certainly a black eye for Teddy, and one that many would find hard to ignore.

In 1924, Teddy was the Republican nominee for Governor of New York. Ironically, his distant cousin, a Democrat by the name of Franklin, was campaigning vigorously for Teddy's opponent, Al Smith. Franklin's wife, Eleanor, was even seen following Teddy's campaign around New York with a steaming teapot strapped to the roof of her car, a not-so-subtle reference to the scandal Teddy had narrowly escaped. Smith won by over 100,000 votes.

Teddy stayed out of the 1928 Governor's race—a campaign won by cousin Franklin; but, Herbert Hoover won the Presidency and promptly appointed Teddy Governor of Puerto Rico. Teddy was a very effective administrator and did much to try and reverse the staggering poverty of the island commonwealth. President Hoover was so impressed with the job Teddy did that, in 1932, he further posted Roosevelt to Governor-General of the Philippines.

Teddy wasn't in that post too long, mainly because Franklin was about to be elected President in Hoover's stead. In late 1932, after FDR's election, he resigned his post and returned home, convinced that his political career was moribund, at least for the time being.

In 1935, Teddy became a senior vice president of the Doubleday Publishing Company and later an executive director of American Express. His business life was flourishing once again, but he never gave up on his dream to reach the Presidency, just like his father. The war clouds that were once again gathering on the horizon might possibly offer him the military glory that he felt he needed to re-ignite his ambitions.

Between the wars, Teddy had continued to attend various reserve officer refresher courses and summer camps, even completing the advanced course at the Command and General Staff College. In 1940, he attended yet another refresher course and was promoted to Colonel in the Regular Army. He returned to active duty in 1941 and was given command of his old regiment, the 26th Infantry. In late 1941, he received his Brigadier General's star, something his father had always coveted but had never achieved. At last, he was finally one step ahead of the "old man."

Roosevelt led his regiment ashore on the coast of North Africa in November 1942. He went in with the first troops to hit the beach. Leading from the front, though frowned upon as military doctrine, was the place you could always find Roosevelt. He was more at home in the thick of things than at some remote command post—a trait he had picked up while in the trenches of France.

By 1943, he had moved up to second-in-command of the 1st Infantry Division under Major General Terry Allen. Allen and Roosevelt were two of a kind: informal, unorthodox, and always somewhere in the middle of the battle. They were not the spit-and-polish, "yes sir" leaders favored by their bosses, the two formidable Lieutenants General, George Patton and Omar Bradley. As a consequence, the pair often ran afoul of their commanders and as a result, both got relieved of their duties after a particularly nasty exchange of words with Patton.

Teddy, however, had a friend in higher places: Dwight D. Eisenhower. Eisenhower put Roosevelt back to work as his liaison with the French Army in Italy during the Sardinia, Sicily, and Italian campaigns. His work was superlative and as a result Teddy got re-assigned to a combat command, this time with the 4th Infantry Division.

The 4th was commanded by Major General "Tubby" Barton, who actually liked Roosevelt a great deal. They worked diligently to get their troops ready to assault Utah Beach on D-Day. Teddy shocked Barton by requesting to go ashore with the troops. Barton initially turned him down. Teddy turned the tables on Barton and put his request in writing: a plea so eloquent that Barton reluctantly relented. Roosevelt would be the only Allied General to go ashore with the first wave of troops. Barton fully expected he would never see Roosevelt alive again.

The assault plan was a good one, but due to some miscalculation in navigation, the entire first wave of the 4th Division landed a mile and a half south of where they were supposed to be. The potential for disaster was immense.

With only a pistol and his walking stick, Roosevelt resolutely climbed the dunes and personally reconnoitered the areas behind the unfamiliar beach. He located all the local causeways and road access points and calmly made his way back to his confused troops. With a totally clear picture of the scene in his mind, he gathered his battalion commanders. He gave them new, clear, and accurate instructions on what to do and uttered the famous phrase, "We'll start the war from right here!"

The first wave stormed over the dunes and onward to success. Roosevelt stayed on the beach coolly directing the succeeding men to where they needed to be. He was under fire the entire time but was often seen acting like a traffic cop, waving his cane overhead, pushing his division forward. When Barton finally got ashore he was greeted by an ebullient Roosevelt, who was still very much alive.

It was a tour de force in innovative and inspirational leadership under fire. Even General Bradley, when asked later in life to name the single most heroic action he had seen during the war, had to admit, "Ted Roosevelt on Utah Beach."

Teddy's friend Barton recommended him for his second Distinguished Service Cross. Eisenhower upped it to the Medal of Honor—and cut orders promoting Teddy to Major General. Sadly, Teddy would not receive either accolade while he was still alive.

The poor health that had dogged him since WW I and the genes he had inherited from his father finally caught up with him. Theodore Roosevelt, Jr., collapsed and died of a heart attack, in France, while leading his troops forward, on July 12th, 1944.

Roosevelt's Medal of Honor was awarded to his family posthumously on September 28th, 1944. Teddy was buried in the American Cemetery in Normandy and after the war, his brother Quentin's remains were moved and placed beside his brother. In two respects, Teddy outdid his father: general's stars and first to receive the Medal of Honor. Incidentally, there have only been two father-and-son recipients of the Medal of Honor: the Roosevelts and the Mac Arthurs: Douglas (WW II) and his father, Arthur (Civil War).

Citation:

"For gallantry and intrepidity at the risk of his life above and beyond the call of duty on 6 June 1944, in France. After 2 verbal requests to accompany the leading assault elements in the Normandy invasion had been denied, Brig. Gen. Roosevelt's written request for this mission was approved and he landed with the first wave of the forces assaulting the enemy-held beaches. He repeatedly led groups from the beach, over the seawall and established them inland. His valor, courage, and presence in the very front of the attack and his complete unconcern at being under heavy fire inspired the troops to heights of enthusiasm and self-sacrifice. Although the enemy had the beach under constant direct fire, Brig. Gen. Roosevelt moved from one locality to another, rallying men around him, directed and personally led them against the enemy. Under his seasoned, precise, calm, and unfaltering leadership, assault troops reduced beach strong

points and rapidly moved inland with minimum casualties. He thus contributed substantially to the successful establishment of the beachhead in France."

Korean War

Chapter 18: Second Lieutenant Sherrod E. Skinner, 2nd Battalion, 11th Marines, United States Marine Corps

Harvard Affiliation: AB, 1951

2nd LT Sherrod Skinner

Midnight, October 26, 1952, in "The Hook," an area of North Korea near the southern border: After a horrific day of attack and counterattack, the forward lines of the 11th Marines were in danger of immediate collapse. Before additional forces could be brought up, a fanatical charge of thousands of Chinese troops, supported by a devastating barrage of rocket, artillery, and mortar fire, temporarily overwhelmed the Marine positions, including the forward observation post of Battery F, 2nd Battalion. The Forward Observer, Second Lieutenant Sherrod Skinner, USMC, had been valiantly rallying those around his trenches for hours. He had called down artillery on top of his own position until his radio was smashed beyond repair. He twice scrambled out of his bunker to help direct machine gun fire against the advancing enemy. He ran back behind the lines and brought up spare ammunition and grenades to the Marines trying to hold their positions. He had been wounded twice and painfully so. He was losing blood and trying to avoid going into shock. Before another rally could be organized, the ammunition finally ran out and the lines were overrun. He told his remaining troops to feign death. The enemy took possession of the forward part of the lines and even searched the men who were pretending to be dead. At several points during the next three hours, the Chinese tossed hand grenades among the Americans. One of these grenades was pitched into a bunker where Skinner and two wounded Marines were desperately trying to avoid discovery and capture. Without hesitation, Skinner rolled on top of the live grenade to shelter his men from the blast. He was killed instantly.

Sherrod Skinner, Jr., was born in Hartford, Connecticut, on October 29th, 1929. His father, Sherrod Sr., was a highly-placed executive at General Motors before and after his son was killed in Korea. Young Sherrod grew up in and around East Lansing, Michigan, went to Milton Academy in Milton, Massachusetts, and entered Harvard in 1947.

In the era immediately after WW II, there was still a great deal of martial energy left in America and many veterans were going back to college on the GI Bill. Patriotic spirit was in vogue at Harvard during those days, and it was not uncommon for underclassmen to volunteer for some sort of military service or training. Sherrod and his twin brother David (who was also attending Harvard) picked the Marine Corps Reserve Platoon Leader's Program.

The brothers went off to active duty during the summers of 1948 and 1949 and soon after graduation in 1951, Sherrod was appointed a Second Lieutenant in the Marine Corps Reserve. By that time, of course, hostilities had broken out in Korea. Sherrod was activated on October 10th, 1951, and sent to Quantico, Virginia, for Marine Corps Officers Basic School.

Immediately after the Basic School, Skinner was ordered to the Artillery School at Fort Sill, Oklahoma. He successfully completed that training in July 1952, then went to Camp Pendleton, California, to prepare for further service in Korea.

Marine Corps second lieutenants are superbly trained and totally indoctrinated in the long, proud history of the Corps, but until they have gained some field experience in a command or leadership capacity, not much in the way of decisive action or demonstrated skill is expected of these un-tested and very junior officers. Sherrod Skinner certainly proved that he had what it took, and exhibited an incredible amount of courage, poise, skill, and effectiveness for someone with so little actual experience.

Sherrod Jr., died three days short of his 23rd birthday, on a barren hill in faraway Korea. His life was far too short, but his courage will live on forever in the annals of great American heroes.

His twin brother David, also a proud Marine Corps veteran, lives, as this book goes to press, in Indio, California.

Citation:

"For conspicuous gallantry and intrepidity at the risk of his life above and beyond the call of duty as an artillery

forward observer of Battery F, in action against enemy aggressor forces on the night of 26 October 1952. When his observation post in an extremely critical and vital sector of the main line of resistance was subjected to a sudden and fanatical attack by hostile forces, supported by a devastating barrage of artillery and mortar fire which completely severed communication lines connecting the outpost with friendly firing batteries, 2d Lt. Skinner, in a determined effort to hold his position, immediately organized and directed the surviving personnel in the defense of the outpost, continuing to call down fire on the enemy by means of radio alone until his equipment became damaged beyond repair. Undaunted by the intense hostile barrage and the rapidly-closing attackers, he twice left the protection of his bunker in order to direct accurate machine gun fire and to replenish the depleted supply of ammunition and grenades. Although painfully wounded on each occasion, he steadfastly refused medical aid until the rest of the men received treatment. As the ground attack reached its climax, he gallantly directed the final defense until the meager supply of ammunition was exhausted and the position overrun. During the 3 hours that the outpost was occupied by the enemy, several grenades were thrown into the bunker which served as protection for 2d Lt. Skinner and his remaining comrades. Realizing that there was no chance for other than passive resistance, he directed his men to feign death even though the hostile troops entered the bunker and searched their persons. Later, when an enemy grenade was thrown between him and 2 other survivors, he immediately threw himself on the deadly missile in an effort to protect the others, absorbing the full force of the explosion and sacrificing his life for his comrades. By his indomitable fighting spirit, superb leadership, and great personal valor in the face of tremendous odds, 2d Lt. Skinner served to inspire his fellow marines in their heroic stand against the enemy and upheld the highest traditions of the U.S. Naval Service. He gallantly gave his life for his country."

Skinner was promoted to First Lieutenant, posthumously.

Vietnam War

Chapter 19: Staff Sergeant Robert C. Murray, 196th Brigade, 23rd Infantry Division, US Army

Harvard Affiliation: Business School, Class of 1970 (1969)

SSG Robert C. Murray

A young man in the prime of his life stares out at us from the photo above. His expression is somewhat bemused, almost a "Mona Lisa" smile. As he turned slightly to gaze into the camera almost fifty years ago what was he thinking? Perhaps something like, "What am I doing in this uniform? This is not what I thought I'd be doing at this point in my life!"

Indeed, Robert Charles Murray, born in Tuckahoe, New York, December 10, 1946, graduated from Fordham University in1968 and applied to Harvard Business School. He was admitted into the Class of 1970. Soon after he finished his first year, single, and quite eligible, his draft notice arrived. Rather than spend more time than necessary fulfilling his military obligation—or avoiding it—he decided to enlist. He would do his duty and move on. He signed up for the Army in New York City and figured he would be out in twenty-four months, then finish Business School, and finally get his MBA.

After basic training and the batteries of tests given to all recruits, the Army determined that Murray was a very bright fellow. He was sent off to Fort Knox, Kentucky and the advanced NCO Academy; colloquially known as "Shake 'N Bake."

By the time his military obligation caught up to Murray, the Vietnam War had ground through thousands of its more experienced mid-level and senior non-commissioned officers. There was a distinct lack of leadership in the Army at these levels. The Army's temporary solution was to take its brightest recruits or draftees and make them "instant NCOs." What these men and women might have lacked in military experience was deemed secondary to their innate intelligence. It was the Army's fondest hope that these "Shake 'N Bakes," would rise to the challenge. Thus it was that Robert Murray, with less than a year's service, found himself a relatively senior E-6 Staff Sergeant as he was shipped off to Vietnam.

When he arrived "in country," on November 7th, 1969, he was quickly detailed to the 4th Battalion, 31st Infantry, 196th Infantry Brigade, 23rd Infantry Division, and assigned as a squad leader in Company B.

On June 7th, 1970, seven months through his twelve-month tour, he and his men were in the Hiep Duc Valley, about thirty-five miles south of Danang. This tortuous valley of dense jungle and intense enemy activity had been dubbed the "Valley of Death." Murray's squad was assigned to search out and destroy an NVA mortar position that had been harassing the Americans.

As they poked and probed through the bush, a member of Murray's squad stumbled on a trip wire attached to a booby-trapped grenade. The soldier froze. If he took another step, or tried to move his foot, the grenade would explode. He shouted to the rest of the men nearby to "Take cover!"

Staff Sergeant Murray, knowing that he and his men were in a dire situation, instantly and unhesitatingly threw himself at the soldier and knocked him aside. Murray fell on the grenade instead, absorbing its full impact. He was killed instantly, without uttering another word.

How easy it would have been to jump the other way, perhaps into the nearby brush or jungle, thereby escaping the powerful blast, or at least most of it. He could have left his man standing on the grenade and moved himself and the rest of his squad to safety—but he did not. As his Medal of Honor citations reads, he acted "instantly...unhesitatingly ...with complete disregard for his own safety."

On August 8th, 1974, Staff Sergeant Murray's family received his Medal of Honor from Vice President Gerald R. Ford at Blair House, in Washington, DC.

Robert Murray did not complete his MBA, of course, or the rest of what could have been his life, but Harvard University and the rest of us will always have his unselfish sacrifice to admire and to honor.

Citation:

"S/Sgt. Murray distinguished himself while serving as a squad leader with Company B. S/Sgt. Murray's squad was searching for an enemy mortar that had been threatening friendly positions when a member of the squad tripped an enemy grenade rigged as a booby trap. Realizing that he had activated the enemy booby trap, the soldier shouted for everybody to take cover. Instantly assessing the danger to the men of his squad, S/Sgt. Murray unhesitatingly and with complete disregard for his own safety, threw himself on the grenade absorbing the full and fatal impact of the explosion. By his gallant action and self sacrifice, he prevented the death or injury of the other members of his squad. S/Sgt. Murray's extraordinary courage and gallantry, at the cost of his life above and beyond the call of duty, are in keeping with the highest traditions of the military service and reflect great credit on him, his unit, and the U.S. Army."

Major McMurtry on his way home from France, after earning
his MOH with the "Lost Battalion"

A "Lost Battalion" Reunion-1939

Lt. Col. Whittlesey receives his MOH-1918

Survivors of the "Lost Battalion" immediately after their rescue

Lt. Col. Pierpont Morgan-1944-wearing his MOH ribbon

Col. Morgan's bravery set the stage for the Americans and the French to unite. In this photo, Maj. Gen. George Patton (r) rides with Gen. Nogues, French commander in North Africa

Brig. Gen. "Ted" Roosevelt-the only general officer to go
ashore in the initial D-Day landings

"Teddy" takes a break with his favorite Jeep--June 7, 1944

A forward artillery position of the 11th Marines, near the
Chosin Reservoir, Korea, where Lt. Skinner earned his MOH

Memorial to Lt. Skinner-dedicated in 2013

Robert C. Murray, Harvard Business School-1969

Only known photo of SSG Murray in Vietnam. As a good
platoon sergeant he is making his men check their feet for
"jungle rot"-a common and serious affliction

Postscripts

Chapter 19: Why?

Of the eight Harvard men awarded the Medal of Honor during the Civil War, seven of them were company, regimental, or brigade commanders in charge of groups of men engaged in spirited actions against a determined enemy (Dr. Curran, as a surgeon, was the exception). It was typical for these men (and many thousands like them) to have viewed the Civil War from the vantage point of standing at the head of a line of thickly massed soldiers who were toe-to-toe with an equally well-armed opposing force. Waving just an ineffective, mostly ornamental sword, these officers faced sheets of deadly lead or canister as their men pounded the opposite line with whatever arms and ammunition they had at their disposal. It took nerves of steel and incredible courage to stand your ground. Survival was based on escaping the thousands of lead balls thrown in their direction, incredible luck, or both. The odds were definitely not in favor of any brave leader.

Why did they do it? How did they do it? Much has been written about the motivation of Civil War soldiers to stand in these long, parallel lines of almost certain death and not waver. Most units were home-grown. The men in many regiments knew each other from connections back home. They had been recruited together, they served together and, if need be, they died together. If they were lucky enough to survive the war, they would go back to the same home towns and anyone who had shirked his duty in some fashion would have had a hard time reintegrating into the communities from whence they had come. The men knew this and no one was anxious to be tarred with the brush of cowardice. It was better to die with honor than to live in shame.

In addition, many Civil War era soldiers had come through the powerful religious revivals of the mid-19th Century. They were imbued with devout Christian teachings about life, death, and the afterlife and the concept of the "Good Death."

As former Harvard President Drew Faust wrote in her award-winning book, *This Republic of Suffering: Death and the American Civil War*:

"Men in Civil War America went to war talking of glory and conquest, of saving or creating a nation, and of routing the enemy. But at the heart of the soldier's understanding of his duty rested the notion of sacrifice." [11]

So, they stood and took the heat of battle, like General Force or Colonel Huidekoper; or, they charged into the middle of it like Blackmar, Phelps, Porter, Stevens, or Lawton. They fully expected to be successful or die trying, and death at the front of your command, doing your duty, was viewed as "a good death," one worth the sacrifice.

In the post-Civil War years, and prior to the enormous set-piece battles of WWI and WWII, America moved through its greatest period of expansion and the fulfillment of its "Manifest Destiny." The military mood shifted from one of laying down one's life for the good of the nation to expanding that nation's boundaries and possessions through daring deeds and military adventure. Thus, we have Leonard Wood heroically carrying dispatches through hostile Indian territory; Theodore Roosevelt charging up San Juan Hill; Walter Hill

---

[11] *This Republic of Suffering*, Faust, Drew Gilpin, New York, Alfred A. Knopf, 2008, pg. 5

storming Vera Cruz; and, Claud Jones valiantly saving the lives of his shipmates during a devastating tsunami.

This was the age of great machismo, when a man was supposed to be a man, when daunting odds and great adventure still went hand-in-hand. If the intrepid hero was fortunate, there would be an article written or a "dime novel" published about his exploits. Then, too, these were still the times when personal courage and physical skill could make a man's fortune.

At the beginning of both WWI and shortly thereafter WWII, America started each conflict with woefully inadequate forces. The United States had standing armies that numbered in the tens of thousands, not the millions that would eventually be required. George McMurtry and Charles Whittlesey were military amateurs; civilians, really, one a stockbroker, the other a lawyer. They were men of courage, however, and deep in the Argonne Forest of France, in 1918, each man led a battalion that endured days of isolated assault, completely surrounded by overwhelming numbers of the enemy. Both men refused offers to surrender honorably. When they were rescued, only a handful of their original troops could walk out of the woods on their own.

Both World Wars were fought against great tyrannies, and both conflicts had profound implications relative to the survival of democracy. Idealism was pervasive and if the will to fight was no longer about personal glory and adventure, the imperative to protect a treasured way of life was strong and deeply ingrained, especially in families with long-standing histories or storied experiences in the American dream.

Both of Harvard's Medal of Honor awardees for WWII came from famous families and both were decorated for storming beaches. In the case of Theodore Roosevelt, Jr., it was his leadership on D-Day, 1944, that caused his superiors to single him out. He sorted through and untangled a logistical and strategic nightmare on Utah Beach during the critical first hours of the invasion. His coolness under fire and his personal bravery prevented a disaster of great proportions.

Pierpont Hamilton waded ashore in North Africa in 1942, braving bullets, bombs, and strafing to get to the commander of the French forces opposing the Americans. His task was to convince the French to surrender without a fight and re-join the Allied cause. He eventually succeeded but not until after several days and a harrowing personal quest.

Neither of these men needed to be where they were. "Teddy" Roosevelt was crippled with arthritis from his service during WWI and had a heart condition (which would eventually kill him shortly after the D-Day landings). Pierpont Hamilton, at age 43, was exempt from service and one of the wealthiest men in America. He could have sat it out.

Sherrod Skinner would throw himself on a live grenade in Korea in 1952, saving two of his men. Robert Murray would do the same thing in Vietnam eighteen years later in 1970. The Korean War wasn't even a war at all and Vietnam was an unpopular and misunderstood conflict, yet these two men, unselfishly and without hesitation, died to save others.

So, then, was there a common denominator among all these heroes? Was it the Harvard tie that bound all of them in an attitude of unstinting patriotism and sacrifice?

The motivations that led to this extraordinary collection of Medal of Honor awardees were very different in almost every case but there is one overriding factor that cannot be ignored, and that factor is the Harvard experience. It is, as everyone who has matriculated at Harvard knows, both a blessing and a burden.

Every single person who has attended Harvard, as an undergrad or grad student (often times both), has heard the response that goes something like this: "Oh! You went to *Harvard*." Many times it is meant as a complement or as a remark of admiration. Sometimes, of course, it is tossed out as a challenge, as in "So, you think you're better than me, eh?" That's what 380 years of tradition and history will generate, along with being perceived as being the best.

The psychology can be studied endlessly and there will be differing conclusions. Personally, this author takes great pride in his Harvard experience and education, and there is no doubt that my time spent in Cambridge was the primary shaping influence of my life. This author also takes enormous pleasure in writing this incredible record of valor—*Crimson Valor*. God bless these men and their courage and may Harvard now and forever continue to produce the men and women who will take up this nation's call to arms and serve so honorably.

Chapter 20: The Military at Harvard Today

In March, 2011, the Naval Reserve Officers Training Program (NROTC) returned to Harvard University after a forty-year hiatus. Harvard's participation in ROTC, in general, was booted off campus unceremoniously in 1969 as a knee-jerk reaction to all things Vietnam. It was a terrible decision, forced on the Harvard community by the anti-war elements that dominated the campus at the time.

Hindsight is always 20/20. The important thing is that the military is back, first with Navy ROTC, followed soon thereafter by both the Army and the Air Force.

The military has never been a primary focus of any aspect of Harvard's educational curriculum; but, it has a proud history on campus nonetheless. The tradition of military service among Harvard alumni had been present even before the Revolutionary War and it stretches all the way forward to every conflict that American arms has ever pursued. The brilliant record of Harvard's association with the Medal of Honor, as chronicled in this book, bears immortal testament to these facts.

At times, the military and Harvard have been powerfully intertwined. We saw this during the Civil War, WW I and especially during WW II, when the Navy's V-12 program practically took over the campus, churning out thousands naval officers for the war effort.

Then, of course, there have been the not-so-obvious interactions in terms of government contracts, weapons research, space studies, scientific exploration with a military focus, and the education of so many active duty officers from all the services over a wide variety of disciplines.

As one small example, this author remembers taking chemistry as a Harvard undergrad. The professor was the chain-smoking, jovial, highly respected Dr. Louis Feiser. I thoroughly enjoyed his class not realizing that this engaging, smiling presence had been the inventor, at Harvard, of napalm, in 1943. That fact was made known to me much later when canisters of the jellied gasoline were strapped under each wing of my fighter bomber.

Harvard and the military are permanently linked in a number of ways, not just in the renewal of officer training. This is a good thing, and here's why: No academic institution with credibility and excellence, like Harvard, should ever be excluded from contact and interaction with the United States Armed Forces. They need each other.

Without a complete and intimate understanding of the military's thinking institutions like Harvard exist in a vacuum of academic isolation without access to military policy and strategy. Courses in government, history, philosophy, politics, biology, chemistry, and physics and a whole slew of other disciplines will be lacking an important element of understanding.

The military, by the same token, needs to be leavened in areas of tactics and strategy by the critical thinking skills and philosophies that are always essential parts of the Harvard educational experience. One can only wonder, for example, what the War in Iraq and the War in Afghanistan might have looked like, from both the tactical and strategic standpoints, if the officer corps, in particular, had been seasoned with more Harvard educated men and women who were part of an uninterrupted ROTC experience during the decades between Vietnam and Desert Storm.

There are markers and reminders of Harvard's military connections all over the campus, from Weld Bridge to Memorial Hall which was built to honor the 176 Harvard men who made the ultimate sacrifice for the Union Cause during the Civil War. [12]

Memorial Church in Harvard Yard was dedicated in 1932 to honor Harvard alumni who served and died during WW I—including the only direct descendant of John Harvard to have ever attended Harvard College.[13] From WW I through the Vietnam War, the names of 1,116 Harvard alumni who have made the supreme sacrifice are inscribed on the walls of Memorial Church: 376 for WWI, 697 for WWII, 18 for Korea, 22 for Vietnam, and 3 graduates of Radcliffe (before its union with Harvard).

The plaque in Memorial Church honoring Harvard's Medal of Honor contains eighteen names, all the names in this book. Will it contain more?

---

[12] The 70 alumni who died fighting for the Confederacy have never been added. There have been at least three serious attempts to do so, but as of this date, all tries have been unsuccessful.

[13] Captain Lionel De Jersey Harvard, Grenadier Guards, British Royal Army, Class of 1915, killed in action, Arras, France, March 30, 1918

Chapter 21: Heroes From the Beginning:

Harvard graduates have mustered under the various banners flown by their countries from the very beginning. While still under British rule Harvard men of Massachusetts (which at the time included Maine) and Connecticut rallied to the cause when the second worst war to take place on American soil erupted in 1675.

King Philip's War, which lasted from 1675-78, started when a Narragansett Indian chief named Metacomet (his English name was Philip), son of the great savior of the Pilgrims, Massasoit, declared war on the New England Colonies in June, 1675. Tensions had been building for several years between the native tribes of New England and the ever expanding, land hungry newcomers. Ironically, the spark that seemed to set off the war was the killing of John Sassamon, the first Native American graduate of Harvard. Sassamon had been acting as a roving negotiator between the two sides, but when he found out Metacomet planned to initiate some raids on selected towns, he reported that information to Massachusetts Governor Josiah Winslow. For this alleged "treason," three Wampanoag warriors ambushed Sassamon, killed him, and dumped his body under the ice of a nearby river.

The Indians were spotted, though, and a witness informed on them. The trio was tracked down by the local militia, put on trial, and hanged. That was the last straw for King Philip.

The war was devastating for both the whites and the native tribes. One-tenth of the male population of the Colonies was killed in the war. Dozens of settlements were burned to the ground across New England. Half the Native American population perished. It was a North American disaster exceeded only by the Civil War almost two hundred years later.

Dozens of Harvard men led companies of militia or went to war as common soldiers. A number of them perished in the skirmishes and stand-up battles that occurred over the war's three years.

And so it went, including Harvard men fighting in King William's War (1689-97); Queen Anne's War (1702-1713); King George's War (1744-48); the French and Indian War, (also known as the Seven Years War) (1754-1763); and, of course, the American Revolution.

Of the 899 Harvard men who fought in the Revolutionary War, 700 took the side of the Colonials, 199 were Loyalists, and 21 Harvard men ended up dead.

According to the extensive research conducted by CAPT Paul Mawn, H-63, and USNR (Ret), "there were 32 Harvard Minutemen at Lexington or Concord in April 1775 and two months later 22 Crimson warriors served in the battle of Bunker Hill. During the arduous six year fight, at least 25 Harvard graduates died while on active duty with the Continental Army: seven were killed in action, four died as prisoners of war and 14 died from diseases or accidents."

As Professor (and later Rear Admiral) Samuel Eliot Morison wrote in his treatise on the War of 1812, Harvard was only "lightly touched" by the so-called Second Revolutionary War. A number of graduates were in uniform, but perhaps the most prominent was Joseph Lovell, AB, 1807; MD, 1811, who served as a surgeon and later became the first Surgeon General of the Army.

The single most noted college "casualty" of that war was the sloop *Harvard*, used to deliver firewood to the university from Maine. In June, 1814, the British captured the ship off the Maine coast and impounded it. The crew was removed safely, and imprisoned in Halifax. The poor *Harvard* was burned and sunk.

The Mexican War (1846-48) was a jingoistic campaign to effect regime change by force of arms, and many good Harvard men ended up sailing off to Mexico with General Winfield Scott. Fewer came back. Exactly how many went and who returned is a subject that has yet to be determined and a task that should be undertaken.

We do know that many of the surviving junior officers--and a few of the senior ones--would gain the experiences necessary to propel them into leadership roles in the coming Civil War.

The Civil War contributions of Harvard men bring us full circle to the beginning of this book. To fill out the record just a bit, consider the following from an insightful article written by Corydon Ireland, for the *Harvard Gazette* in March, 2012:

"Late on the afternoon of Sept. 4, 1861, the soldiers of the 20th Massachusetts Volunteer Regiment, fresh and eager for action after six weeks of training, boarded trains in Readville, Mass. They were headed south, to war.

"The 20th was called 'the Harvard regiment' because so many of its officers were educated at the College. Some had left Harvard as undergraduates, quitting school in April when the first rebel shells rained down on Fort Sumter. By 1865, the regiment's nickname was "the Bloody 20th." Of the nearly 3,000 Union regiments that saw action, the Harvard regiment had the fifth-highest number of casualties.

"Harvard faculty, undergraduates, and graduates served in other regiments as well, and in every branch of the service. There were 246 dead among the 1,662 with Harvard ties who fought on both sides. In the Union ranks, 176 died. On the Confederate side, where 304 men with Harvard connections enlisted, 70 died, a mortality rate two and a half times higher than the Union side."[14]

Of the roughly 700 men on those train cars leaving from Readville, only 44 would survive the war.

The total so-called "butcher's bill" (a term attributed to Capt. Oliver Wendell Holmes, Jr., of the 20th Massachusetts), for Harvard ended up looking like this:

Union enlistments: 1,358
College, 608
Medical School, 387
Law School, 285
Lawrence Scientific, 54
Divinity, 23
Observatory, 1

Killed or died of wounds, 110
Died from disease, 63
Died from accidents, 3

Confederate enlistments: 304
College, 94
Medical School, 2
Law School, 177
Lawrence Scientific, 31
Killed or died of wounds, 57
Died from disease, 12
Died from accidents, 1

---

[14] Ireland, Corydon, "Blue, gray and Crimson," *Harvard Gazette*, March 21, 2012

Eighteen year old 2nd Lieutenant Sumner Paine, Class of 1865, was mortally wounded at Gettysburg. He was the youngest Harvard man to die in the war. His last words were, "Isn't this glorious?"

Chapter 23: On the Pyramid of Honor: Harvard Alumni and the Distinguished Service Cross (DSC); Navy Cross (NC); and the Air Force Cross (AFC)

By 1916, The Army and Navy realized they had a public relations challenge on their hands as well as no effective way to reward acts of valor and courage that were bold or brave but didn't rise to the level of MOH recognition.

As outlined in Chapter 1, a Medal of Honor Review Board was convened by Congress in 1916 to review all of the 2,625 MOH awards (19 of which were second awards) handed out to that date. The Civil War had generated 1,520 awards, the Indian Wars offered up another 443. The Spanish-American War, Vera Cruz (1914), and a smattering of non-combat, peacetime awards (fair game under the old rules) had generated another 662.

Over 900 awards of the MOH were rescinded. Some were easy decisions: one Union colonel, who had never come close to seeing any qualifying action simply requested a MOH and it was sent to him. The 29 soldiers who escorted Lincoln's casket from Washington, DC, to Illinois were given MOHs. Those were rescinded. One was given to a British citizen, whose actions had merit, but he was a foreigner and ineligible. Another soldier had put out a warehouse fire, and one other trooper had simply delivered a message, and not under fire. Five MOHs for Cavalry scouts were rescinded because the awardees were civilian contractors. The 864 awards mistakenly granted the 27th Maine Regiment were also retracted.

New and more stringent requirements were put in place, and the procedures tightened up. There was also a limitation added that an individual could only receive one MOH.[15]

The service chiefs also agreed that an array of additional awards were necessary, and thus began the design and promulgation of dozens of new combat medals, campaign ribbons, and non-combat awards.

Beginning in 1918, the MOH was placed atop a "Pyramid of Honor," which would consist of additional hierarchical awards for valor. The second highest awards in the Pyramid became "the Crosses:" For the Army, a Distinguished Service Cross (DSC) was initiated (1918). For the Navy, Marine Corps, and Coast Guard, the Navy Cross was authorized (1919). The Army Air Service and Army Air Corps members who were deemed worthy received the DSC until the US Air Force was established and a an Air Force Cross was created in 1960.

From WWI until today, hundreds of Harvard alumni have been awarded the DSC, Navy Cross, or Air Force Cross. Like the MOHs chronicled in this book, these awards display an astonishing array of brave deeds and courage under fire. It would take hundreds of pages to tell all these stories, and that is beyond the scope of this catalog. Instead, it was decided to offer a few sample stories of the actions of some of the alumni who have been honored with one of "the Crosses."

The Harvard Hall of Heroes on the website of the Advocates for Harvard ROTC lists bios and many pictures of almost 200 Harvard veterans who were recipients of major valor awards some of which are described herein.

---

[15] For example, US Army retired Col. Robert Howard was nominated three times for the MOH for his service in Vietnam. He received one MOH from President Nixon and the other two nominations were downgraded to awards of the Distinguished Service Cross.

WW I:

One-hundred two Harvard alumni were awarded a total of 113 DSCs or Navy Crosses during WWI and of those men, 23 were killed in action.

The following stories were selected at random by the author to serve as representatives of the valor and courage of all of these men:

Class of 1896: Captain John Chamberlain Ward: US Army, 108th Infantry, 27th Division: The 45-year-old Ward, an Episcopal Bishop, was exempt from military service because of his age, but he volunteered as a chaplain anyway and sailed for France in May, 1918. He participated in the Somme Offensive that summer and fall. He earned a DSC as a "battlefield angel," as set forth in the following citation: *"For extraordinary heroism in action east of Ronssoy, France on 29 September, 1918. During operations against the Hindenburg Line, Chaplain Ward, voluntarily and at a great risk to himself, went forward under heavy shell and machine gun fire to care for the wounded and to search for the dead. Twice he was ordered off the field of battle by officers, being told each time that it was sure death to remain. During the entire time his regiment was engaged he remained on the field under fire, displaying a fine example of bravery and courage which was an inspiration to all"*. After the war he returned to the ministry in Buffalo, New York, until he retired in 1943. He promptly volunteered, again, for military service in WW II; but, at age 69, this time he was firmly but politely rejected.

Class of 1899: Major Dwight F. Davis,[16] US Army, 69th Infantry, 35th Division: As a Harvard student, he won the American intercollegiate tennis singles championship of 1899 and earned the men's tennis singles title at the US Championships in 1898 and 1899. A news account described Davis as "tall, dark, and keen, without an ounce of superfluous flesh," and the *Crimson* once dubbed him the "Harvard Cyclone" due to his "slam-bang aggressive" style. Left-handed and a big server, he thrived on net play and had probably the most crushing overhead of his era. In 1900, Davis developed the rules for and donated a silver bowl to go to the winner of a new international tennis competition later renamed the Davis Cup in his honor.

After Harvard, Davis graduated from Washington University Law School but never became a practicing attorney. He returned to his home town of St. Louis where he was active in both civic affairs and politics.

In the summer of 1915, he attended the initial Plattsburg Military Camp for businessmen in upstate New York. When the US entered World War I in 1917, Davis was commissioned as an Army officer in the infantry. After shipping out to France, he participated in the St. Mihiel and Meuse–Argonne Offensives for which he was awarded the DSC for his heroism as noted in the following citation: *"The Distinguished Service Cross is presented to Dwight F. Davis, Major (Infantry), U.S. Army, for extraordinary heroism in action between Baulny and Chaudron Farm, France, September 29 - 30, 1918. After exposure to severe shelling and machine-gun fire for three days, during which time he*

---

[16] Davis was in the same graduating class as Maj. George McMurtry, MOH recipient, whose profile appears in Chapter 14.

displayed rare courage and devotion to duty, Major Davis, then adjutant, 69th Infantry Brigade, voluntarily and in the face of intense enemy machinegun and artillery fire proceeded to various points in his brigade sector, assisted in reorganizing positions, and in replacing units of the brigade, this self-imposed duty necessitating continued exposure to concentrated enemy fire. On September 28, 1918, learning that a strong counterattack had been launched by the enemy against Baulny Ridge and was progressing successfully, he voluntarily organized such special duty men as could be found and with them rushed forward to reinforce the line under attack, exposing himself with such coolness and great courage that his conduct inspired the troops in this crisis and enabled them to hold on in the face of vastly superior numbers".

After the War, Davis returned to St. Louis until he was appointed as Assistant Secretary of War (1923–25) and then the Secretary of War (1925–29) by President Calvin Coolidge. Under Herbert Hoover, he then served as Governor General of the Philippines (1929–32). During World War II, he was the Director General of the Army Specialist Corps until his death in Washington, DC, in November of 1945.

Class of 1902: Major Edward Ball Cole USMC, 6th Regiment, 2nd Division: In 1904, he was commissioned a lieutenant in the US Marines and served at sea as well as ashore on bases in the United States, Philippines, Puerto Rico and Mexico. For several years before World War I, he trained in machine guns and became a leading expert in their use and deployment. He sailed for France in December, 1917, as the commanding officer of the 6th Machine Gun Battalion. After serving on the front line in the Verdun area, he moved to the

Phil Keith

Chateau Thierry area and then the hellish action at Belleau Wood. His Navy Cross citation reads: *"In the Bois de Belleau, France on 10 June, 1918, his unusual heroism in leading his company under heavy fire enabled it to fight with exceptional effectiveness. He personally worked fearlessly until he was mortally wounded"*. His DSC citation reads: *"In the Bois de Belleau on 10 June 1918, he displayed extraordinary heroism in organizing positions rallying his men and discharging his guns, continuing to expose himself fearlessly until he fell. He suffered the loss of his right hand and received wounds in upper arm and both thighs"*. He was also awarded the Legion d'Honneur and the Purple Heart.[17]

Class of 1910: Private Saxton Conant Foss, US Army, 9th Infantry, 2nd Division: After graduating from Harvard, he worked as a reporter for the *Christian Science Monitor* and the *Boston Globe*. He enlisted in June 1917 and did not seek "preferment" to enter officer training camp. He sailed to France later than summer and was soon involved in hard, continuous, fighting in several areas including the Saint-Mihiel and Champagne offensives of 1918. Nearly every night, he was sent out on patrols to explore "No Man's Land" and often served as a runner between companies.

In the Saint-Mihiel offensive, he was killed in action after he volunteered to flank a machine gun nest that was holding up his advancing battalion. His DSC citation reads: *"For extraordinary heroism in action near Medeah Farm, France, October 8, 1918. With exceptional courage, Private*

---

[17] In the WWI period, an individual could be awarded both the DSC and the Navy Cross for the same heroic act. This was particularly true for Marines fighting with or alongside US Army units. The practice was discontinued after the war.

Foss voluntarily advanced to flank a machine gun nest unaided which was holding up the advancing battalion and in so doing was fatally wounded."

Class of 1910: Lt. Leon Magaw Little, US Navy, Armed Guard Commander: Little was commissioned an Ensign in the Massachusetts Naval Militia and transferred to the US Navy on the battleship *USS Nebraska.* In April, 1917, he was re-assigned as the Armed Guard Commander on a US commercial tanker (the *SS Joseph Cudahy).* To combat the devastating losses being experienced by US flag shipping at the hands of Germany's u-boats, President Wilson, in 1916, had authorized the deployment of teams of US Navy sailors aboard civilian merchant ships, and the equipping of these ships with one or two 3-inch naval guns. It was as the commander of the *Cudahy* Detachment, in November, 1917, that Little and his men valiantly dueled with two German u-boats determined to sink their ship. Little's heroics resulted in a Navy Cross as detailed in the following citation: *"For distinguished service in the line of his profession as Commander of the Armed Guard of the SS Joseph Cudahy, and in encounters with enemy submarines. On 17 November 1917, a periscope was sighted and the ship fired nine shots, when the submarine disappeared, again reappeared, when six more shots were fired, and finally disappeared. In November 1917 at night, sighted a submarine close aboard, attempted to ram and fired three shots, when gun jammed. The submarine then disappeared."*

Class of 1910: 1st Lt. George Buchanan Redwood, US Army, 28th Infantry, 1st Division: After Harvard, he studied in

Germany for a summer and then returned to Baltimore to work as a broker and later as a reporter for the *Baltimore News*. In the summers of 1915 and 1916, he attended the Reserve Officer training camp at Plattsburg, NY. In August, 1917, Redwood was promoted to 1st Lt. in the regular Army and sailed for France in September. He trained at the British 4th Army School for scouting, sniping, and observation from which he graduated as an intelligence officer in December. Lt. Redwood participated in several combat engagements in the Ansauville sector where he earned the first of two DSCs: *"For extraordinary heroism in action at Seicheprey, France, March 1918. With great daring he led a patrol of our men into a dangerous portion of the enemy trenches, where the patrol surrounded a party nearly double their own strength, captured a greater number than themselves, drove off an enemy rescuing party, and made their way back to our lines with four prisoners, from whom valuable information was taken.*

He was later awarded an oak-leaf cluster for his second DSC, as noted in the following citation: *"For the following act of extraordinary heroism at Cantigny, France on 28 May, 1918, he conducted himself fearlessly to obtain information of the enemy's action. Although wounded, he volunteered to reconnoiter the enemy's line, which was reported to be under consolidation. While making a sketch of the German position on this mission he was under heavy fire, and continued his work after being fatally wounded until it was completed. The injuries sustained at this time caused his death"*. He was also awarded the Croix de Guerre.

Master of Arts, 1911: Captain James N. Hall: US Army, 3rd Pursuit Group, Army Air Service: Hall initially enlisted as a private in the 9th Battalion, Royal Fusiliers (British Army) in August, 1914, claiming he was a Canadian. After fighting at the Battle of Loos, his true citizenship was discovered and he was honorably released from the British Army. In December 1915, he then enlisted as a private in the French Foreign Legion and later received aviation training at French Army Air schools. After 18 months, he was assigned to Squadron N124 (Lafayette Flying Corps) as a brevet pilot. Soon thereafter he was shot down and wounded. After a brief recovery period, he transferred to the Squadron SPAD 112 and finally back to Squadron N124 where he was promoted to pilot-sergeant in December 1917. Hall was honorably discharged from the Foreign Legion in February, 1918, and immediately commissioned as a captain in the US Army Aviation Section of the Signal Corps and assigned to the 103rd Squadron. Captain Hall was again wounded and this time taken a prisoner of war for eight months. Hall was released after the end of the war. He is officially credited with the destruction of three enemy airplanes. His DSC citation reads:

"In March 1918 while leading a patrol of three, Captain Hall attacked a group of five enemy fighters and three enemy two-seaters, himself destroying one and forcing down two others in a fight lasting more than twenty minutes."

After the war Hall moved to Tahiti where he spent most of the rest of his life writing. His most famous work, with co-author Charles Nordhoff, was "Mutiny on the Bounty."

Class of 1911: Lt. General Hanford MacNider, US Army, 9th Infantry, 2nd Division: Born in Mason, Iowa and educated at Milton Academy before entering Harvard, he was an editor of the Harvard Crimson and a member of the Hasty Pudding Club. After graduating from college, he joined the Army National Guard and soldiered in the Pancho Villa Expedition in Mexico in 1916. During WWI, as a captain, he participated in the following engagements: Chateau-Thierry, Aisne defensive, Marne-Aisne offensive, Marbache sector, Saint-Mihiel offensive, Champagne offensive (Blanc-Mont Ridge) and the Meuse-Argonne offensive. His first DSC citation reads: (for September 12, 1918): *"On duty as regimental adjutant, while carrying instructions to the assaulting lines, he found the line unable to advance and being disorganized by a heavy machine-gun fire. Running forward in the face of the fire, this officer captured a German machine gun, drove off the crew, reorganized the line on that flank, and thereby enabled the advance to continue".*

As a newly promoted lieutenant colonel, MacNider was awarded an oak-leaf cluster in lieu of a second DSC, for the following: *"For extraordinary heroism in action near Medeah Farm, France from 3 to 9 October 1918. He voluntarily joined an attacking battalion an October 3, and accompanied it to its final objectives. During the second attack on the same day he acted as runner through heavy artillery and machine-gun fire. He visited the lines both night and day, where the fighting was most severe. When higher authority could not be reached, he assumed responsibilities and gave the necessary orders to stabilize serious situations. When new and untried troops took up the attack, he joined their forward elements, determined the enemy points of resistance by personal observation.*

MacNider returned to the US and was discharged from active duty in September, 1919. MacNider served as the

National Commander of the American Legion in 1921, and later was appointed as Assistant Secretary of War under President Coolidge and then the US ambassador to Canada by President Hoover in 1930. During World War II, and promoted to brigadier general, he commanded the 32nd Infantry Division and was wounded in the Buna Invasion of New Guinea in November, 1942, for which he received his 3rd DSC. He retired from the Army in 1951 as a major general but was then appointed to Lieutenant General by Act of Congress. MacNider was also awarded the Croce al Merito di Guerra (Italy), three Silver Stars, two Bronze Stars, two Purple Hearts and the Philippine Legion of Honor.

Class of 1914: 1st Lt. Charles Warner Plummer, US Army, 101 Forward Artillery and 88th Aero Squadron: After graduating from Harvard, he worked for the Northwest Mutual Life Insurance Company in Boston and simultaneously served in Battery A of the Massachusetts Field Artillery. He was activated for service on the Mexican Border (1916) and was federalized and commissioned as a 2nd Lt. in July, 1917, sailing for France two months later. He was transferred to the aviation service in January 1918 and was trained in several French aviation schools as an aerial gunner and observer. He was awarded the Croix de Guerre by Marshall Petain who wrote in the citation: "*July 24, 1918, while protecting a group of aviators over the enemy line, he* (i.e. 2nd Lt. Plummer) *engaged in a combat with several German planes. During the combat, he received more than 30 bullets in his plane but continued to fire and succeeded in beating off his adversaries.*"

He was in in the Vesle sector (Fismes) when he was killed in action on August 11, 1918, while on a hazardous photographic mission with other planes in his squadron. He aided in driving off over a dozen German aircraft and was materially responsible for the successful execution of the mission. His DSC citation, signed by General John Pershing, states: "*2ⁿᵈ Lt. Charles W. Plummer, Observer, 101ˢᵗ F.A. distinguished himself by extraordinary heroism in connection with military operations against an armed enemy of the United States at Fismes, France on 11ᵗʰ August 1918 and in recognition of his gallant conduct, I have awarded him in the name of the President, the Distinguished Service Cross.*"

Class of 1914: Captain Willard Smith, US Army, 9ᵗʰ Infantry Regiment, 2ⁿᵈ Division: After graduating from college, he worked at the F. S Mosley brokerage firm in Boston and at the same time served as a non-commissioned officer in Battery A of the Massachusetts National Guard. During the summers of 1915 and 1916, he participated in the Reserve Officer training camp at Plattsburg, NY. During the winters of the same two years, he attended the Military Officer Training School at the Charlestown Armory. Rather than become a captain in the National Guard, he accepted a commission in the Regular Army as a 2ⁿᵈ Lt. He sailed for England in September, 1917, and then crossed immediately over to France. Due to his proficiency in French, he was temporarily made the military mayor of a French town before being assigned command of the regimental supply company. He was killed in action on September 12, 1918, at Saint-Mihiel, France. His DSC citation reads: "*For extraordinary heroism in action near Remenauville, France* *on 12 September 1918. Lt. Smith was killed while gallantly assisting in maintaining liaison between the troops advancing on the open ground to the west of the Bois de Four. It was due to Lt. Smiths' fearless example while leading his men that the line was held intact at this point.*" Smith was posthumously promoted to captain.

Class of 1915: Sergeant Dana Newcomb Trimble, US Army, 1st Engineers, 1st Division: Trimble enlisted in the Army and was immediately promoted to corporal in May, 1917. He sailed for France in August, 1917, where he was promoted to sergeant in April 1918. After being wounded three months later, he was hospitalized in France until shipped back to the USA in May, 1919. His DSC citation reads: "*For extraordinary heroism in action near Soissans, France during July 1918. He volunteered and obtained the consent of his company commander to recover wounded men from an exposed area in front of the line. He went through a violent bombardment in the performance of this duty three times and stopped only when he himself had been severely wounded.*"

Class of 1916: 2nd Lt. Kenneth Eliot Fuller, US Army, Company C, 23rd Infantry: Fuller came from Exeter, NH, born in 1894 and the son of lawyer who had graduated from Harvard in 1877. Both grandfathers, a great- grandfather and a great-great grandfather were Harvard alumni. His grandfather, Arthur Buckmaster Fuller (H-1843) was chaplain of the 16th Massachusetts Volunteers and was killed at the battle of Fredericksburg. Kenneth earned letterman "H's" on the varsity cross country and track teams. After graduating cum laude, he entered Harvard Law School participating in Officer Training Camp at Plattsburg, NY, in May, 1917. He was commissioned a 2nd Lieutenant in the infantry in August. After further training in the US, he set sail for France in April, 1918. He initially was assigned as a judge advocate in Headquarters in Tours, France and could have remained indefinitely in this billet but he requested an infantry unit on the front lines, near Chateau–Thierry. He was killed in action on July 18, 1918, when his regiment lost 62 officers and 1,922 enlisted in a single mission. These brave American troops had to attack many well placed German machine gun nests with only pistols and rifles. In the process, they broke through the German lines and captured 75 German officers and 2,100 enemy soldiers. His DSC citation reads: *"For extraordinary heroism in action near Vaux-Casiille, France on 18 July 1918. When his company was temporarily halted by heavy machine gun fire, 2nd Lt. Fuller personally led a group of ten men in an attack on the machine gun position. He was killed while leading this attack, but due to his heroic example, the enemy position was captured and his company was able to continue its advance"*. 2nd Lt. Fuller also was posthumously awarded the Croix de Guerre by the Republic of France.

Class of 1916: Lt. (j.g.) David Edward Judd US Navy, Attached to the Northern Bombing Group, Royal Air Force: He initially volunteered as an ambulance driver in the American Field Service with the French Army on the Argonne and Champagne fronts from January to July, 1917. He then enlisted as a private in the French Foreign Legion and subsequently transferred to the French Aviation Service. He was designated as a pilot in October, 1917, and assigned to Squadron 73 (Lafayette Flying Corps) in December, 1917. He was honorably discharged from the French Army in January, 1918. He was immediately commissioned as an ensign in the

US Naval Reserve and assigned to US Naval Air Station, Dunkirk, France. A month later, he transferred to the Northern Bombing Group. His Navy Cross citation reads: *"For distinguished and heroic services as an aviator in an aeroplane engaged in active operations with the Allied Armies on the Belgian Front during September, October and November 1918, bombing enemy bases. Aerodromes, submarine bases, ammunition dumps, railroad junctions etc."* Judd returned United States in September, 1918, and served as flight instructor until he was released from active duty in February 1919.

Class of 1917: Captain Douglas Campbell, US Army, 94th Aero Squadron: Campbell sailed for France in July, 1917, and was wounded in June 1918. He returned to the US for recuperation and sailed again to France in November 1918. Captain Campbell became an "ace," officially credited with the destruction of six enemy planes. He was in the same squadron as Medal of Honor recipient and top "ace," Captain Eddie Rickenbacker. His first DSC citation: *"For extraordinary heroism in action on 19 May 1918. He attacked an enemy biplane at an altitude of 4,500 meters, east of Flirey, France. He rushed to attack, but after shooting a few rounds his gun jammed. Undeterred by this accident, he maneuvered so as to protect himself, corrected the jam in midair and returned to the assault. After a short, violent action, the enemy plane took fire and crashed to the earth."*

In addition, one bronze oak leaf is awarded Lt. Campbell for the additional DSC citation for each of the following acts of heroism in action. On 17 May 1918, he encountered 3 monoplanes at the altitude of 3,000 meters over

Montsec, France. Despite superior strength of the enemy, he promptly attacked and fighting a brilliant battle, shot down one German machine, which fell in 3 pieces and drove the others well within enemy lines. On 28 May 1918, he saw 6 German Albatross aeroplanes flying towards him at an altitude of 3,000 meters near Bois Rata, France. Regardless of personal danger he immediately attacked and by skillful maneuvering and accurate operation of his machine gun, he brought one plane down in flames and drove the other 5 back to their own line. On 31 May 1918, he took the offensive against 2 German planes at an altitude of 2,500 meters over Lironvitte, France, shot down one of them and pursued the other far behind German lines. On 5 June 1918, accompanied by another pilot, he attacked 2 enemy battle planes at the altitude of 5,700 meters over Elpy, France. After a spirited combat, he was shot through the back by a machine gun bullet, but in spite of his injury he kept on fighting until he had forced one of the enemy planes to the ground where it was destroyed by artillery fire and had driven the other plane back into its own territory.

Class of 1917: Lt.(j.g.) George Thomas Roe, US Navy Attached to the Royal Flying Corps (British): He enlisted as a seaman 2nd class in May, 1917, and was assigned to the Naval Aviation detachment at MIT. After flight school at Pensacola, FL, he received his wings of gold as a Navy aviator and was commissioned an ensign. He went overseas in January, 1918, where he was assigned to fly with the Royal Air Force in the UK. He was shot down and was a prisoner of war from May to December 1918. After the war, he was transferred to the US Naval Air station near Cork, Ireland, for a few months before returning to the United States in February 1919. He finished his Harvard degree in 1920 but died while on active duty in San Diego, CA, in May 1921. His Navy Cross citation reads: *"For distinguished service and extraordinary heroism as an Aviator attached to the British Royal Air Force. Participated in many offensive patrols over the North Sea. On May 30th, 1918, the sea plane in which Ensign Roe was second pilot made a forced landing in the North Sea, owing to engine trouble. While the crew was engaged in making temporary repairs, five enemy sea planes appeared and opened fire. Ensign Roe and his companions heroically returned the fire and continued the fight until two of the crew had been killed and three were knocked overboard. After destroying their machine, the remaining survivors were picked up by the German sea planes and taken to the enemy base at Barken, where they were made prisoners of war."*

Class of 1918: 1st Lt. Alfred Wild Gardner, US Army, 305th Infantry, 77th Division: He joined the Harvard regiment as a sophomore and in 1916 went to the first ROTC encampment at Plattsburg, NY. In May, 1917, he was commissioned a 2nd Lt. of infantry and sailed for France in April, 1918. His convoy was attacked by German submarines but he safely reached Liverpool and then departed immediately for Calais, France. After extensive training in Scouting, Observation, and Sniping School and Gas School, he moved up to the front lines. He led several successful combat excursions in "No Man's Land" and became company commander when his CO was killed. On October 3, 1918, he was ordered to lead a frontal attack against a hill full of German machine gun nests. His DSC citation reads: *"For extraordinary heroism in action in the Argonne Forest, France on 3 October 1918. Attacking enemy machine gun nests, he displayed the highest courage* *when he led his company up a steep slope in the face of murderous fire. Before he could accomplish his objective, he was killed."*

Class of 1918: Captain Clifford West Henry, US Army, 102nd Infantry, 26th Division: As a senior, he applied for a year's absence to go into the Army. After his commissioning, he was assigned to the 46th Division and sailed for France in July, 1917. After serving temporarily with the 104th Marines, Henry was assigned to the 26th (Yankee) Division. On 14 September in the Verdun sector, St. Mihiel, he was mortally wounded in the stomach by a high explosive shell which also killed his commanding officer and 50 of his men. He died a month later from these wounds. At the time, he was engaged to Margaret Mitchell, author of "Gone with the Wind." His DSC citation reads: *"For extraordinary heroism on 14 September 1918. During the Saint-Mihiel offensive, although mortally wounded and suffering great pain, he gave information for the disposition of his men. He refused first aid until other wounded men had been taken care of".*

Class of 1919: 1st Lt. Francis Reed Austin, US Army, 109th Infantry, 28th Division: He enlisted in the Army in January, 1918, and three months later sailed for France on a ship which was almost torpedoed by a German submarine. In the 305th Infantry Division, he was initially promoted to sergeant and later commissioned as a 2nd LT and transferred to the 109th infantry. Austin's tragedy is simply unique and an incredible instance of bad timing. He was killed on the last day of the war, fifteen minutes before the last shot was fired. His DSC citation reads: *"For extraordinary heroism in action east of Haumont, France on 11 November 1918. He led a platoon of* *machine guns and two 1 pounder guns with their crews under cover of fog within the enemy's wire and attacked at close range a strong point held by 25 men and 10 machine guns. After this position had been reduced, concentrated machine-gun fire from the ranks forced Lt. Austin and his party to withdraw. Exposing himself in order to place his men under cover, he was mortally wounded but directed the dressing of the wounds of his men and their evacuation before he would accept any aid for himself. He died a few hours later".*

Class of 1919: Captain Hamilton Coolidge, US Army, 94th Aero Squadron, 1st Pursuit group: He was born in Chestnut Hill, MA, in 1883, a great-great-grandson of Thomas Jefferson. He was one of eight children of Joseph Randolph Coolidge (H-1883) who had four of five sons on active duty in the war. He prepped at Groton for Harvard where he was on the football and baseball teams. He received his pilot license in the summer of 1916 after civilian training in Buffalo, NY. He enlisted in March 1917 and sailed to France in July 1917 with his close friend Quentin Roosevelt. He tested planes for a few months before joining a combat unit but by September, 1918, he had become an "ace" with an official credited destruction of five enemy airplanes and three balloons. General Pershing himself wrote Captain Coolidge's DSC citation. *"For extraordinary heroism in action near Grandpre, France on 27 October 1918 . Leading a protection patrol, Captain Coolidge went to the assistance of two observer planes which were being attacked by 6 German machines. Observing this maneuver, the enemy sent up a terrific barrage of anti-aircraft guns on the ground. Disregarding the extreme danger, Captain Coolidge dived straight into the barrage and his plane was struck and sent down in flames."* Coolidge, who was killed in the action described above, was also awarded the Croix de Guerre from France and the Purple Heart.

Class of 1919: Lt. (j.g.) William Gaston, US Navy, Northern Bombing Squadron, RAF: Gaston was born in Boston in 1896 and prepped at St Marks for Harvard. His grandfather was a former mayor of Boston and governor of Massachusetts. His father (H-1880) was a classmate of President Teddy Roosevelt and a partner in the family law firm of Gaston & Snow. Gaston was called to active duty in May, 1917, and initially assigned to NAS Squantum, MA, before reporting to Hampton Roads, VA, where he was commissioned as an ensign and later qualified as a naval aviator. After aerial gunnery school in Fort Worth, Texas, he sailed for Europe in March, 1918, with orders for duty with the Royal Naval Air Force (RNAF) at the Hornsea Base (England). He was subsequently sent to the RNAF School of Navigation and Bomb Dropping in Stonehenge (England) where he later became an instructor. His next assignment in June 1918 was with the US Northern Bombing Squadron in France. Based on his bravery for actions flying with the British Navy, Gaston was awarded a Navy Cross whose citation reads: *"The President of the United States of America takes pleasure in presenting the Navy Cross to Lieutenant Junior Grade Gaston United States Navy (Reserve Force) for distinguished and heroic service as an Aviator operating with the U. S. Naval Aviation Forces Foreign Service and with the British School of Night Bombing. Lieutenant Gaston made several raids over enemy lines."*

Class of 1919: 1st Lt. David Putnam, US Army, 139th Pursuit Squadron: Putnam was a direct descendent of General Israel Putnam of American Revolutionary War fame. During freshman year, he passed the exams for aviation service but was rejected for being too young. He took a job on a cattle ship to Europe and went to Paris and enlisted as a private in the French Foreign Legion. In May, 1917, thanks to his aviation training, he was sent to French flight school. After graduation and brevetted a pilot, he was assigned to Escadrille SPAD 94 at the front and later transferred to the Lafayette Escadrille. He was honorably discharged as a sergeant in the French Army in June, 1918, and immediately commissioned a 1st Lt. in the US Army Aviation Service. He served a short stint on the front as (temporary) commanding officer of the 134th Pursuit Squadron. In his year of active duty in both the French and US Army Aviation, he became an "ace" officially credited with 14 victories. He was the only American to shoot down five German planes in one day. He was killed in action just over 16 months after enlisting in the French Foreign Legion and four months after his commissioning into the US Army. His DSC citation reads: *"For extraordinary heroism in action near La Chaussée, France on 12 September 1918. After destroying one of the 8 German planes which had attacked him, he was turning to our lines when he saw 7 Fokkers attack an allied biplane. He attacked the Germans and saved the biplane but was himself driven down, shot through the heart."* Lt. Putnam also received six awards for valor from the French Republic including the order of the Chevalier in the Légion d'Honneur, the Médaille Militaire, and the Croix de Guerre.

WWII

The list of Harvard warriors earning the nation's second highest awards, during WWII and beyond, is still a work in progress. So far we have discovered the records for fifteen citations of which there are twelve awards of the Navy Cross, two awards of the DSC, and one award of the Air Force Cross. If anyone reading these pages knows of another Harvard alum who belongs in this category, the author would be most grateful to receive your information so that we can record these deeds of valor in subsequent revisions.

Class of 1930: Major James Roosevelt, USMC, 2nd Marine Raider Battalion**:** James Roosevelt was the oldest child of Franklin and Eleanor Roosevelt. Prior to WWII, the younger Roosevelt had served as a personal secretary to his father in the White House and had been given a (controversial) commission in the Marines as a lieutenant Colonel in 1936; controversial because Roosevelt had no military training or experience whatsoever. When WWII broke out, to prove his true mettle, Roosevelt resigned his lieutenant colonel's commission and accepted a much lower ranking captain's commission in the Marines and volunteered for combat. And prove his valor, he did, as Executive Officer of the newly formed 2nd Marine Raider Battalion, in the August, 1942, raid on Japanese held Makin Island. His Navy Cross citation reads as follows: *"The Navy Cross is presented to James Roosevelt, Major, U.S. Marine Corps (Reserve), for extraordinary heroism and distinguished service as second in command of the Second Marine Raider Battalion against enemy Japanese armed forces on Makin island. Risking his own life over and above the ordinary call of duty, Major Roosevelt continually exposed himself to intense machine-gun and sniper fire to ensure effective control of operations from the command post. As a result of his successful maintenance of communications with his supporting vessels, two enemy surface ships, whose* *presence was reported, were destroyed by gun fire. Later during evacuation, he displayed exemplary courage in personally rescuing three men from drowning in the heavy surf. His gallant conduct and his inspiring devotion to duty were in keeping with the highest traditions of the United States Naval Service."*

Roosevelt also was awarded a Silver Star for gallantry in action in the Gilbert Islands in November, 1943. After the war, he settled in California and went into private business, then served almost six terms in Congress as a Representative of California's 26th District.

Class of 1932: LT James H. Gaul, US Navy, 277th Battalion, OSS: Gaul was as serious and studious as they come, earning an AB, MS, and a PhD in Anthropology, all from Harvard, by 1940. He taught at Boston College before answering his country's call for service in WWII. He joined the Navy as an intelligence officer in 1941 and served two years in the Middle East before transferring to the newly incorporated Office of Strategic Services (OSS). Without hesitation, he agreed to infiltrate German occupied Czechoslovakia in 1944 along with a group of OSS operatives. Their mission was to assist the Slovak insurgents and rescue downed Allied airmen forced to parachute into their area. The team was highly successful until a determined effort by the German Army tracked almost all of them down. Fourteen OSS men, including LT. Gaul, were transported to the German concentration camp at Mauthausen, Austria. All were tortured, and then in January, 1945, each was lined up, in turn, against a wall and shot by firing squad, including the brave LT. Gaul. The remains of these brave men have never been found. Even though a Navy man, Gaul was awarded a posthumous DSC since at the time of his death he was serving with a unit affiliated with the US Army. His citation reads as follows: *"The President of the United States of America takes pride in presenting the Distinguished Service Cross (Posthumously) to James Harvey Gaul, Lieutenant, U.S. Navy (Reserve), for extraordinary heroism in connection with military operations against an armed enemy while serving with Company B, 2677th Regiment, Office of Strategic Services, in action in action against enemy forces from 17 September 1944 to 26 December 1944. Lieutenant Gaul's outstanding accomplishments, personal bravery and zealous devotion to duty exemplify the highest traditions of the military forces of the United States."*

After the war, LT. Gaul and his teammates were honored with a "plaque for the missing" at the Epinal American Cemetery in France.

Class of 1938: LCDR Brent Maxwell Abel, US Navy, Commanding Officer, *USS Buckley*, DE-51: Brent Abel majored in French at Harvard, then after graduation went to Harvard Law School from which he graduated with his law degree in 1940. He moved to San Francisco to practice tax law and estate planning. When WWII broke out, he volunteered immediately. Having been a member of NROTC at Harvard, he was already a reserve lieutenant, junior grade. After a year of training in Corpus Christi, Abel, promoted to lieutenant, was made commanding officer of a sub chaser escorting convoys into the Atlantic. In early 1943, promoted once more to lieutenant commander, Abel was selected as the first commanding officer of the *USS Buckley*, DE-51. The *Buckley* was the lead ship of a new class of destroyer escorts which would ultimately include 102 hulls launched in just an incredible two-year time span. The *Buckley* was a hunter-killer ship whose primary mission was the detection and destruction of enemy submarines. In the early morning hours of May 6, 1944, (Captain Abel's 28th birthday) the Buckley was alerted by the escort carrier *USS Block Island*, CVE-21, that a German u-boat had been sighted nearby. The *Buckley* raced to the scene and what unfolded over the next few hours was an astonishing, swashbuckling, tale of sea-going derring-do that maybe the most unique single ship action in all of WWII.

After visually sighting the *U-66,* the *Buckley* charged ahead, straight at the sub, somehow avoiding the u-boat's torpedoes and the shells from its 3-inch surface gun. Firing its own 20-mm and 50-caliber guns, the *Buckley* peppered the deck and conning tower of the sub then literally rammed the boat, the bow of the destroyer riding right up on the after deck of the u-boat, and sticking there.

With the two ships locked together in a death grip, the crew of the u-boat clambered out of the forward hatch and conning tower and swarmed over the bow of the *Buckley*, intent on boarding and doing battle with the Navy crew. The men of the *Buckley* responded in kind, and bearing pistols, iron bars, boat hooks, coffee cups, and shell casings, went at the German sailors in hand-to-hand combat.

Captain Abel gave the order for "emergency back full," and the *Buckley* screeched and groaned off the back of the sub. The u-boat was then freed and although mortally wounded, managed to swing around and smash into the hull of the *Buckley*, ripping open a gaping hole in the hull along the starboard side. The u-boat bumped and swung around further, smashing into the *Buckley's* fantail. American sailors took advantage of the sub's proximity to toss hand grenades into *U-66's* open hatches. This was the coup de grace for the *untersee* boat.

U-66 began to sink. *Buckley* managed to rescue 36 of the sub's crew and then transferred them to the *Block Island* before Capt. Abel headed for the Brooklyn Navy Yard for repairs.

The dramatics of Capt. Abel and his crew generated both a Navy Unit Commendation for the Buckley and a Navy Cross for Abel, as set forth in the following citation: *"The President of the United States of America takes pleasure in presenting the Navy Cross to Lieutenant Commander Brent Maxwell Abel, United States Navy, for extraordinary heroism and distinguished service in the line of his profession as Commanding Officer of the Destroyer Escort USS BUCKLEY (DE-51), in offensive action against a German submarine. While patrolling the Atlantic Coast on the early morning of 6 May 1944, Lieutenant Commander Abel expertly directed his command and made an undetected, high-speed approach in bright moonlight to a surfaced German U-boat. With skilled seamanship, he silenced its guns within four minutes after contact, despite a heavy barrage of enemy torpedo and automatic weapon fire. Narrowly escaping another torpedo, he then closed on the wildly maneuvering submarine, raked it with all available fire and rammed, with the enemy attempting to board the vessel in retaliation. Withstanding the desperate attacks of the enemy ship, which tried to ram after the combatants became disengaged, he persistently held to his target until the submarine, with its conning tower shattered and burning fiercely, all hatches open, abandoned by its crew and completely out of control, disappeared beneath the surface of the water and exploded. His conduct throughout was in keeping with the highest traditions of the Navy of the United States."*

Capt. Abel's heroics became the basis for the 1957 film "The Enemy Below," starring Robert Mitchum and Curt Jurgens. Abel went back to his law practice and also stayed in the Naval Reserve after the war, retiring as a full Captain.

Class of 1938: LT Joseph P. Kennedy, Jr., US Navy, Patrol Squadron 203, Bombing Squadron-110, Special Air Unit One (Europe): Joe Kennedy, the eldest son of Joseph P. Kennedy, Sr., and Rose Kennedy--and older brother to future President John F. Kennedy--was in his first year at Harvard Law School when he decided to delay his law degree to join the US Navy in April, 1941. He trained as a naval aviator, received his wings, and was assigned as a patrol plane pilot in 1942. He flew 25 combat missions over the Atlantic in 1942-43, and was eligible for a return to a "safe" assignment stateside, but turned that down to volunteer for "special missions" involving remote controlled bombers, in England. Perhaps he was a bit envious of his younger brother, Jack, also a navy officer, who had won fame and a hero's status as commander of fabled PT-109 in the South Pacific. Jack had a Navy and Marine Corps Medal and a Purple Heart. Joe had not earned more than a couple of campaign ribbons--and nothing significant for "valor." The story is fairly well known, but Joe volunteered for "Operation Anvil," an early and very experimental use of drones or non-piloted aircraft to bomb hazardous enemy installations. Specially modified US Navy PBY patrol planes and B-24 "Liberator" bombers were used as the airframes.

They would be stripped down of all excess equipment then stuffed to the gills with highly explosive torpex or C-4 explosives. Very brave aviators like Kennedy volunteered to be the "take-off pilots." These experimental flying bombs needed human help to get off the ground. Once in the air, and the package armed, the live pilots would bail out over friendly territory. The then un-manned planes would continue on to their targets, guided by a radio controlled signal from a chase plane.

On August 12, 1944, LT. Kennedy and his co-pilot took off in a B-24 whose 2,100 pound munitions package was intended to land on the German u-boat pens in Helgoland in the North Sea. Two minutes after arming the package (Kennedy radioed that he had done so) and five minutes before the pilots were to bail out, the plane suddenly and unexpectedly exploded in midair. The B-24 and the crew were instantly obliterated. No cause for the tragedy was ever discovered.

Of the 15 experiments with these manned/un-manned drones, not a single mission was even slightly successful. The project was finally abandoned in January, 1945.

LT. Kennedy was posthumously awarded the Navy Cross, Distinguished Flying Cross, and the Air Medal. Kennedy's Navy Cross citation reads as follows: *"The President of the United States of America takes pride in presenting the Navy Cross (Posthumously) to Lieutenant Joseph Patrick Kennedy, United States Navy, for extraordinary heroism in operations against the enemy while serving as Commander of a Navy Liberator Patrol Plane in Bombing Squadron ONE HUNDRED TEN (VB-110), Special Air Unit ONE (Europe), during a special air mission directed at Mimoyecques, France, on August 12, 1944. Well knowing the extreme dangers involved and totally unconcerned for his own safety, Lieutenant Kennedy unhesitatingly volunteered to conduct an exceptionally hazardous and special operational mission. Intrepid and daring in his tactics and with unwavering confidence in the vital importance of his task, he willingly risked his life in the supreme measure of service, and, by his great personal valor and fortitude in carrying out a perilous undertaking, sustained and enhanced the finest traditions of the United States Naval Service."*

Class of 1940: Captain Theodore Woods Noon, Jr., 351st Infantry, 88th Division, US Army: Ted was born in Cambridge where he graduated from Rindge Tech prior to Harvard. His DSC was earned for his heroics as a rifle company commander in Italy in 1944. Before and after the war, he worked in Oklahoma as a petroleum engineer and geologist with Texaco. After his MBA from HBS, he became an investment banker in Boston and New York. For his Harvard 25th reunion report, Ted stated: "My job in Italy was to take hills without stopping to study the geology and to lose as few men as possible". He retired to New Hampshire with his wife Marjorie in 1978. His DSC citation reads as follows: *"The President of the United States of America, authorized by Act of Congress July 9, 1918, takes pleasure in presenting the Distinguished Service Cross to First Lieutenant (Infantry) Theodore Woods Noon, Jr. (ASN: 0-1285480), United States Army, for extraordinary heroism in while serving with the 351st Infantry Regiment, 88th Infantry Division, in action against enemy forces on 12 and 13 May 1944, near Santa Maria Infante, Italy. While advancing in an attack, First*

Lieutenant Noon was severely wounded in both arms by machine gun fire; but in spite of his wounds he rushed an enemy pill box and single-handedly knocked a machine gun out of action. During this engagement he received several wounds on his face and head, but returned to his company and led his men forward to take the objective. Refusing to be evacuated for medical treatment, Lieutenant Noon led his company in an attack against another enemy position. While making a personal reconnaissance, he was wounded in both legs by shell fragments. Again refusing aid, he ordered the officers with him to return to the company and start the attack. In the last phase of the attack First Lieutenant Noon had recovered sufficiently to lead his men forward in the assault. When the objective was taken, he personally supervised the reorganization of his company. Only upon the order of his superior officer did he allow himself to be evacuated for hospitalization. First Lieutenant Noon's courage under fire, his prodigious determination, and his aggressive leadership were an inspiration to his men, and his heroic performance reflects the finest traditions of the Armed Forces of the United States.

Harvard Business School AMP, 1968: Colonel (later Brigadier General) Robert F. Titus, 389th Tactical Fighter Squadron, US Air Force: A career Air Force officer, Titus was commissioned a second lieutenant in 1949. After distinguished service in many assignments, and steady promotion to colonel, he was sent to Vietnam in 1966. In May, he assumed command of the "Skoshi Tigers," the only F-5 squadron in the U.S. Air Force, at Bien Hoa Air Base. In January 1967 he became commander of the F-4-equipped 389th Tactical

Fighter Squadron at Da Nang Air Base. He flew 400 combat missions in North and South Vietnam and destroyed three Mig-21s in aerial combat. In September 1967 General Titus was assigned to Headquarters U.S. Air Force, where he was project officer for the F-15 and chief of Advanced Tactical Systems in the Office of the Deputy Chief of Staff, Research and Development. He entered the National War College in August 1969. In June 1970, he went to MacDill Air Force Base, Fla., as vice commander, 15th Tactical Fighter Wing and later became commander. He retired in 1977 with the rank of brigadier general. His Air Force Cross citation reads: *"The President of the United States of America, authorized by Title 10, Section 8742, United States Code, takes pleasure in presenting the Air Force Cross to Lieutenant Colonel Robert F. Titus (AFSN: 0-26472), United States Air Force, for extraordinary heroism in military operations against an opposing armed force as an F-4C Mission Commander in the 389th Tactical Fighter Squadron, 366th Tactical Fighter Wing, Danang Air Base, Vietnam, in action near Hanoi, North Vietnam, on 22 May 1967. On that date, Colonel Titus led his flight into one of the most heavily defended areas of North Vietnam in direct support of F-105 strike aircraft operations. Undaunted by accurate flak and five surface-to-air missiles that were launched at his aircraft, he repeatedly and unhesitatingly engaged numerous MiG-21s in defense of the friendly aircraft. During these aggressive and courageous aerial encounters, Colonel Titus destroyed two MiG-21 aircraft. As a direct result of his tenacity and extreme bravery in the face of great danger, the F-105 force was able to accomplish its assigned mission. Through his extraordinary heroism, superb airmanship, and aggressiveness in the face of hostile forces, Lieutenant Colonel Titus reflected the highest credit upon himself and the United States Air Force.*

Chapter 24: Valor Abounds

Below "the Crosses," "Stars" were established. The third highest award for valor is the Silver Star (1932) and the fifth highest combat award is the Bronze Star (1944).

The highest valor awards given strictly for flight operations are the Distinguished Flying Cross (1926) and the Air Medal (1942) which fall at fourth and seventh place, respectively, in the Pyramid of Honor.

Rounding out the very top awards for personal actions in combat situations is the country's oldest medal, the Purple Heart. Originally initiated by George Washington as a valor award, the medal was revived in 1932 and re-designated as an honor to be given to all veterans who were either wounded or killed "In combat against an enemy of the United States."

A catalog of the Silver Stars, Bronze Stars, Purple Hearts, Distinguished Flying Crosses, and Air Medals earned by Harvard alumni would take several hundred more pages. Suffice it to say that the men and women of Harvard who have patriotically donned any of their country's uniforms have made their alma mater extremely proud. Service to the nation via the military is a common thread throughout the Harvard experience. Sometimes, as in the Vietnam Era, that thread has been all too thin and stretched to the point of unraveling. Sometimes, as in WWI and WWII that thread has widened to a broad blanket of protection in which to wrap the nation. Thick or thin, however, the bond has held and has never broken. Harvard and the alumni who have embraced the flag via military service should be very proud.

<u>Acknowledgements</u>

A special thank you to Capt. Paul E. Mawn, USNR-Ret., for his inspiration. Paul graduated from Harvard with a degree in Geology in 1963. While at Harvard, he joined NROTC and immediately upon graduation was commissioned an ensign and went on active duty. He served in amphibious ships and destroyers, and qualified as a Surface Warfare Officer. Upon release, he stayed in the Navy Reserve and completed a total of twenty-eight years of combined active and active reserve duty, retiring as a Navy captain. Along the way, Captain Mawn accumulated a host of awards and was decorated with the Navy Commendation Medal for his service on active duty during Desert Storm.

In civilian life, Paul is president of Concord Consulting Group, with significant experience as both a senior line manager and consultant in the petroleum industry.

Paul gave me the initial impetus for this book. He is a tireless supporter of both his alma mater and the military and was instrumental in bringing recognition of Harvard's Medal of Honor awardees to the attention of a grateful university—and the nation.

Captain Mawn is the current Chairman of the Advocates for Harvard ROTC which had over 2,600 Harvard Alumni members, most of them military veterans. The Advocates were the "point of the spear" for the resumption of ROTC on Harvard's campus, after a forty-year hiatus.

Paul's herculean efforts, as well as the work of many others, came to fruition with the signing of a new NROTC pact between Harvard and the Department of the Navy in 2011. "Well done," Captain, and thank you for your devoted leadership.

Another special thank you to Tom Reardon '68 for his tireless support of the Military Community at Harvard. He served as an Infantry platoon leader in Vietnam, receiving the Combat Infantryman Badge and the Bronze Star. In 2005, Tom founded the Harvard Veterans Alumni Organization, which continues to successfully press for the admission of more ROTC candidates and young Veterans to Harvard College. HVAO also prepared and donated the Medal Of Honor commemorative plaque to Memorial Church in Harvard Yard.

Last but not least I must mention the courageous leadership of former Harvard president Drew Gilpin Faust whose foresight and persistence made the difference in the resumption of ROTC programs at Harvard.

About the Author:

Phil Keith holds a degree in history from Harvard. He attended on an NROTC scholarship and was a Distinguished Naval Graduate. Immediately after college, Phil was commissioned, went on active duty in naval aviation, and after receiving his wings was sent to Naval Justice School. Phil served three combat deployments to Vietnam and was awarded a number of combat decorations and campaign citations. He retired from the active Naval Reserve after 22 years of service.

Phil has authored three fictional novels and seven nonfiction books to date. His two Vietnam books are both from St. Martin's Press: *"Blackhorse Riders"* won the 2012 USA Book News award for Best Military Non-Fiction, was a finalist for the 2013 Colby Award and earned a Silver Medal from Military Writers Society of America. His second Vietnam book, *"Fire Base Illingworth,"* was released in 2013. *"Stay the Rising Sun,"* (Quarto Publishing, 2016) is an account of the crucial WW II Battle of the Coral Sea and the loss of the aircraft carrier *USS Lexington* in May, 1942. *"Stay the Rising Sun"* won a Bronze Medal from The Military Writers Society and was a finalist for the 2016 Morison Award for Naval Literature. *"All Blood Runs Red"* the biography of Eugene Bullard, the first African-American fighter pilot (co-written with best-selling author Tom Clavin), under contract to Hanover Square Press, will be released in November 2019. Hanover Square has also contracted with Phil and Tom Clavin to produce another work of non-fiction, *"To The Uttermost Ends of the Earth,"* the riveting story of the Civil War's most famous sea battle, the duel between the *USS Kearsarge* and the *CSS Alabama* (to be released in early

2021). Phil has also completed a biography of Maj. Gen. Henry W. Lawton, one of the eighteen Harvard Medal of Honor recipients entitled "Long Hank," the manuscript is currently out for bid.

Phil serves on the planning board for the Town of Southampton, writes an award-winning column for the Southampton Press, and is a member of VFW Post 5350, American Legion Post 924, the Disabled American Veterans, and Vietnam Veterans of America.

"I live full-time in Southampton with my wonderful partner, Laura Lyons, and my terrific son Pierce, and I am extremely proud to be both a graduate of Harvard and a veteran of the United States Navy."

Phil Keith

Made in the USA
Lexington, KY
25 November 2019

57663071R00109